Also by John D. Williams Jr.

Everything SCRABBLE ® (with Joe Edley)

Dispatches from
the Games, Grammar,
and Geek Underground

JOHN D. WILLIAMS JR.

LIVERIGHT PUBLISHING CORPORATION

A DIVISION OF W. W. NORTON & COMPANY

Independent Publishers Since 1923

New York · London

"Scrabbling over Scrabble" by Stefan Fatsis, from the *New York Times*, July 14, 2013. All rights reserved. The printing, copying or retransmission of the content without expressed written permission is prohibited.

For information about permission to reproduce selections from this book, write to Permissions, Liveright Publishing Corporation, a division of W. W. Norton & Company, Inc., 500 Fifth Avenue, New York, NY 10110

For information about special discounts for bulk purchases, please contact W. W. Norton Special Sales at specialsales@wwnorton.com or 800-233-4830

Manufacturing by Quad Graphics Fairfield
Book design by Ellen Cipriano Design
Production manager: Julia Druskin

Library of Congress Cataloging-in-Publication Data

Williams, John D., Jr.
Word nerd : dispatches from the games, grammar, and geek underground / John D. Williams, Jr. — First edition.
pages cm
ISBN 978-0-87140-773-3 (hardcover)
1. Scrabble (Game) I. Title.
GV1507.S3W55 2015
793.734—dc23

2015009100

ISBN 978-1-63149-190-0 pbk.

Liveright Publishing Corporation
500 Fifth Avenue, New York, N.Y. 10110
www.wwnorton.com

W. W. Norton & Company Ltd.
Castle House, 75/76 Wells Street, London W1T 3QT

1 2 3 4 5 6 7 8 9 0

to Jane Ratsey Williams and George Merritt

CONTENTS

FOREWORD

OVER THE YEARS, PEOPLE'S REACTION TO my work has always been a blend of bemusement and bewilderment.

"You may quite possibly have the most random job in the United States," a *Los Angeles Times* reporter once told me.

"I bet you're a really good speller!" at least 372 different people have remarked to their own amusement at various social gatherings.

"I hate you. And if you insist on taking words like *asshole, cunt* and *spic* out of the SCRABBLE® Dictionary, you're going to be sorry. I know where you live, and what you look like." This note was received from a disgruntled—and anonymous—word lover who had read a news story about the proposed "cleansing" of the *Official SCRABBLE Players Dictionary.*

"Dad, next time can you please walk behind me?" That was my thirteen-year-old daughter as we passed three boys from her class on the sidewalk in our small town. "Hi, Mr. SCRABBLE!" the boys had shouted to me.

"John, this is a business. If you want to keep doing this, you have to think more like a marketing person and less like a SCRABBLE player," a senior Hasbro Games executive told me in a meeting.

"John Williams cares nothing about the game and tournament players. I bet he doesn't even play SCRABBLE! He's only in it for the money." That was posted by a West Coast veteran tournament player on a popular gamer website. A quick check of the official tournament statistics page revealed my SCRABBLE rating was almost 200 points higher than hers!

"My wife and I have played a game of SCRABBLE every night for 47 years. I honestly think it's keeping us alive! Thank you," a man from Ohio wrote.

"We have to always remember that this game is bigger than all of us." That was from my wife and business partner, Jane Ratsey Williams.

Okay. That's what some other people have said. Now it's my turn.

1

THE GAME BEGINS

WHEN I WAS SIXTEEN YEARS OLD, my parents summoned me into the small den of our suburban home on Long Island. They sat me down opposite them and proceeded to outline a plan.

"Look, John, we all know that your sister is the smart one," my father began as my mother nodded in agreement, "so we've had to make a family decision about college. Your mother and I have agreed that we have to save our money so your sister can go to a well-known, prestigious school."

He then produced an envelope and withdrew five brochures. They were all from small, private men's colleges, each located in the middle of nowhere in Virginia, New England, or Pennsylvania and each with a bargain-priced tuition. It was up to me to select one.

Four years later, when I was twenty, my parents followed up that earlier confidence builder with a second sit-down in the same spot. My father's tone was pretty much the same as well.

"John, we need to be honest with each other here," he started out. "By almost any criteria you've pretty much underperformed in college. For openers, you went from being a National Honor Society student at a very competitive suburban high school to a C student in college."

My mother was not going to be left out this time. Fortified by a couple of martinis, she jumped in. "You screwed around too much. You're completely irresponsible with money. You're very immature."

While I'd like to say those accusations were unfounded, the truth is they were not formed in a vacuum. So I said nothing.

"Since this is your senior year in college," my father continued, "it's time to discuss the best plan for you after graduation."

My best bet, he said, was to find a large company that was willing to give me a chance. Once there, I needed to make sure that I did whatever they told me, showed up on time every day, and kept my mouth shut. "And don't be a wise guy," he added.

"Just follow that plan, and you'll have no problems," my mother urged. "Then you stay at that company for thirty or forty years. So when you're sixty-five, they'll take care of you until you die."

I remember considering their advice. For about five minutes. This book is about what I did instead.

I'll do us both a favor and bypass the early work experiences: the lemonade stand, the lawn mowing, the paper route. We've all done some variation of these tasks—designed to teach us the value of a dollar, project management, and other realities of working for or running an organization.

Moving forward, I need to clear up a couple of things. First, to the best of my knowledge and recollection, everything described in this book really happened over the last thirty years in the world of SCRABBLE. That said, there are a couple of disclaimers. For example, in some cases I've changed names or completely left them out when legally necessary.

I've also changed the venue in a couple of places—from a boardroom to a restaurant, from Chicago to Los Angeles, that kind of thing. That's pretty much it. Oh yeah, I should also say that I suffer no illusions about my own role in all these stories. I have it on good authority from a disturbingly large and well-credentialed roster of people that the case could be made that at times I was overconfident, clueless, evasive, lazy, political, and dead wrong. And, of course, all the observations and opinions expressed in this book are mine only.

Mostly, though, I'm proud of what I've accomplished and experienced. I am humbled by the people I've met and worked with. They include famous authors and journalists, numerous celebrities, brilliant game players, legendary word nerds, corporate CEOs, television and movie executives, my own colleagues at the National SCRABBLE Association (NSA), kids in the National School SCRABBLE Program, and so many more. All of them had critical roles in our collective mission to first revive a sagging SCRABBLE brand and then craft a plan to ensure the future of this glorious game. And I'm thankful for all the remarkable people I've met and worked with and the wild, random adventures this job afforded me.

I'm thankful as well for the spectacular work atmosphere I enjoyed all those years. My office was in an old sea captain's house on the East End of Long Island, almost exactly a hundred miles from midtown Manhattan. At the height of the NSA's activities, there were ten of us working there, the women outnumbering men two to one. Depending on the day, there were also as many as three dogs hanging around. We had a screened-in porch where we held our summer meetings and a kitchen where soup was invariably being made in the winter. The phone rang constantly; many days we fielded well over fifty calls. They ranged from people wanting us to settle a dispute over a rule or word to someone asking us to send a ninety-year-old lifelong SCRABBLE fan a birthday letter to a Hasbro executive asking for input on a new game idea.

Ironically, very little SCRABBLE was played on the premises during the workday. We were too damned busy. Among our core responsibilities:

- Overseeing the activities of more than two hundred official SCRABBLE clubs throughout North America
- Scheduling and sanctioning nearly three hundred SCRABBLE tournaments annually
- Publishing the *SCRABBLE News* eight times a year
- Maintaining the official tournament rating system
- Coordinating up to seventy-five literacy fund-raising events annually
- Working with publisher Merriam-Webster on updating the *Official SCRABBLE Players Dictionary*
- Reviewing SCRABBLE book manuscripts and new product ideas for Hasbro
- Searching the media and Internet for SCRABBLE knock-offs and trademark violations
- Overseeing the National School SCRABBLE Program and doing outreach to schools, parks and recreation

departments, educational conventions, libraries, and
more

■ Organizing and promoting the National SCRABBLE
Championship, the National School SCRABBLE
Championship, and the World SCRABBLE Champion-
ship

■ Serving as technical advisers when SCRABBLE was
used in a film, television show, or commercial

2

OPENING MOVES

I KNEW VIRTUALLY NOTHING ABOUT SCRABBLE WHEN I began this adventure. I did come from a family of word and game lovers, but my gaming pursuits at the time were poker, crossword puzzles, trivia, and backgammon.

When I say I come from a family of word lovers, I should confess that we came from the darker side of the word world: grammar. Yes, grammar, that purist pursuit that engenders, if not outright encourages, endearing personal qualities such as self-righteousness, pedantry, and a sense of superiority. In our household, should any family member misuse or mispronounce a word, he or she could pretty much count on the correct usage being shouted out instantaneously, often by more than one other person. Forty years after the incident, my family still chuckles smugly about the time my uncle Richard blurted out the word IRREGARDLESS when telling a story. Clearly, he had mistakenly blended REGARDLESS with IRRESPECTIVE. Still, he was hooted out of the room, bolting in a flustered huff. Sadly, Uncle Richard did not live to see that IRREGARDLESS is now included in *Merriam-Webster's Collegiate Dictionary, Eleventh Edition.*

It's important for those of us in the Grammar Police to examine our motivation:

- Is it to make the world a better-communicating and more ear-pleasing place?
- Is it to help a friend or loved one avoid an embarrassing grammar situation in the future?
- Is it simply to satisfy our own need to be right?
- Is it a means to show someone up—a boss, an enemy— by making ourselves look smarter?

Only you and your conscience know your true motivation. However, the Grammar Police in my family defused any negative accusations by employing this mantra: it's not about being right, it's about being *accurate.*

Ultimately, this topic raises the question of what to do in daily conversation when confronted with an appalling misuse or mispronunciation of a word or phrase. The more tolerant of us will simply shrug it off—perhaps silently and complacently noting the transgression—and move on. Others, with a fervent commitment to pristine language and, perhaps, a dark personal need, have a number of options.

One is *correctly using the mangled word or phrase a bit later in the same conversation.* Let's say your neighbor uses the word BANAL while telling a story, mispronouncing it as "*bay*-nul" as opposed to the preferred "buh-*nal.*"

After wincing, you allow the story to continue. Then, after

the topic has moved on, you find a way to use the word yourself later on in the conversation, pronouncing it correctly. At that point, you've done all you can. The onus is on your neighbor to recognize the transgression.

Option two: *just flat-out call the offender on it.* As I said, my family would simply shout out the correct usage or pronunciation in the culprit's face, a gleeful Greek chorus of the self-righteous. There is, however, a tamer and arguably more practical and sensitive approach than that brutal tactic. I confess to employing it exactly once in my life.

A colleague of mine, well educated and highly successful in business, was telling a story about attending a very high-profile, black-tie charity affair. A modest guy, he remarked about his fascination and slight discomfort at "being there hobnobbing with all the HOI POLLOI."

I immediately knew his intended meaning: that he was among the upper class. Sadly, the actual meaning is the complete opposite, and I was dismayed—for him—by his unfortunate choice of phrase. Of course, we are all guilty of sprinkling our conversations with the occasional foreign phrase, right? It's an efficient and time-tested technique to subtly display our intellect and sophistication. Or so we'd like to think.

My sense was that he might have been thinking of "HOITY-TOITY," a similar-sounding phrase with a slightly foreign tinge. It has a secondary meaning of "highfalutin." Regardless, something possessed me to stop my friend dead in his tracks with this question.

"Excuse me, Max, but if you were misusing a word in conversation, would you want me to tell you?" When I told another word-loving friend about this later, he eloquently replied, "Dude, how the fuck is he supposed to answer that question!" He maintained that my approach could be classified as nonviolent social aggression.

At any rate, Max allowed that of course he'd want to know if he was misusing a word. I was even certain I detected a sliver of gratitude in his reply. Before I corrected him, I explained that I myself am the kind of person who would definitely want to know as opposed to going through the rest of my life unwittingly offending language sticklers—and looking stupid. Later, I decided upon reflection that this approach was both impractical and socially dangerous. That left me with no choice but to consider the third option: *the anonymous letter.*

While this option may seem a bit of overkill and of dubious character, it is effective. I hasten to add that I've never actually employed this tactic. However, an example might be along these lines.

Dear Brenda:
You are one of the smartest and most wonderful people I know, and I treasure our relationship. However, I need to write to you about an important matter that's been going on for some time. There's no easy way to tell you this, but I've noticed a number of times that you've been misusing the words LIE, LAY, and LAIN and I feel compelled to call it to your attention. Please know that, according to experts, these are among the most misused words in the English language. So don't beat yourself up too much! I just thought you'd want to know.

Sincerely,
A friend

The benefit here is twofold. First, you've successfully removed one more instance of incorrect word usage from the atmosphere. Second, you've helped a friend—whether it was asked for or not.

In addition to my family's word and grammar vigilance, my early life was subject to an authority of an even higher order—the Roman Catholic Church. This dynamic operated on two levels. First, the traditional English curriculum—taught at my all-boys school by grim, presumably celibate monks—was disproportionately devoted to language, vocabulary, and reading. To this day, should a syntax emergency arise, I could effectively diagram a sentence to avert a disaster. At least I like to think so.

I remember one time, in fifth grade, being whipped with the knotted rope belt worn around a monk's waist for a reading mistake. I was standing in front of a class of fifty boys, reading aloud a passage about Monaco. I kept saying "prince-abil-ity" instead of "princ-*ipal*-ity." Six times I mispronounced the word, and six times the rope lashed the back of my thighs. Finally, I was sent to my seat in shame. The monk immediately called up another boy, who promptly read it correctly, punctuating it with a gloating smirk in my direction.

I got off easy. A year later, a teacher hung one of my classmates out a third-story window by his ankles for using the word "ain't."

But the church did contribute to my word nerdom in other ways. For example, I was an altar boy. This meant that as a ten-year-old I had to learn hundreds of words and phrases in Latin in order to serve Mass. Understandably, this contributed to a lifelong curiosity about words. Later, four years of Latin in high school helped me understand the value of Latin roots as well. It also developed an ability to memorize hundreds of words that served no purpose whatsoever in the real world—a very useful skill for SCRABBLE players. The reality is that no one is going to go very far in the world of tournament SCRABBLE who isn't willing to commit to memory obscure but tile-valuable words.

Here's an example of such a word: UMIAQ. Every tournament SCRABBLE player knows UMIAQ. It means "an Eskimo canoe" and is also spelled with a K: UMIAK. It's of interest because it is one of just three words in the English language that has a Q and U that are not connected. The others are QIVIUT, which means "the wool of a musk-ox," and BURQA, an alternative spelling of BURKA. Pretty obscure stuff, huh? Yet one day, many summers ago, I received an excited telephone call from my friend and frequent SCRABBLE opponent Herb Scannell, who at the time was president of Nickelodeon. He had just returned from a vacation to Iceland. His excitement was palpable through the long-distance connection.

"You'll never guess what I just saw on my trip!" Herb gushed. "I was leaving the airport in Greenland. About a mile outside of the exit, I spotted a sign nailed to a tree. In big letters, it said 'Umiaq for Rent'!"

"No shit! You're kidding me!" I was excited as he. This was a word nerd's version of people seeing the image of the Virgin Mary on a piece of toast or a tree stump. Only after he hung up did I realize that I'd forgotten to ask whether it was the UMIAQ or UMIAK spelling. In the spirit of full disclosure—and to head off angry letters and calls—I should mention that UMIAQ has additional alternative spellings. Among them are OOMIAC and OOMIACK.

■ ■ ■

It's probably the single question I've been asked the most over the last twenty-five years. "So how does one get to be the executive director of the National SCRABBLE Association?" Of course, the subtext to that question is often "Why you?"

I can't speak for anyone else, but here's how it happened for me. I *literally* can't speak for anyone else, because I'm the only one who's ever had the job. However, there was an official organization before the National SCRABBLE Association that went by the catchy name of SCRABBLE Brand Crossword Game Players, Inc.

The earlier organization was an in-house division of Selchow & Righter, then the SCRABBLE trademark holder and manufacturer. It was a relatively small, family-owned company, best known for SCRABBLE and Parcheesi. The SCRABBLE Brand Crossword Game, Inc., unit was comprised of a company executive with a couple of assistants. No one in the organization admitted to being an accomplished SCRABBLE player, nor were any tournament players actively involved in the running of the organization.

At the time, 1982, I was working out of our house in the country, trying to write a novel and doing advertising and public relations for a couple of clients both locally and in New York City. My brother-in-law worked at advertising giant J. Walter Thompson in Manhattan, where Selchow & Righter was a client. As often happens in that business, a colleague of his, John Nason, was leaving to move over to the "client side" to become the vice president of marketing for Selchow & Righter. As Nason's new job would be on Long Island, about an hour from my home, it was suggested we meet.

John Nason and I hit it off immediately. He was a thoughtful, smart, elegant man, who had cowritten an excellent book on advertising entitled *Advertising: How to Write the Kind That Works*. He was looking to form alliances in his new job and suggested that I might be able to contribute to the fledgling *SCRABBLE Players Bulletin* published by his company.

That's how it all started. I then spent a couple of years working with Nason's colleague Jim Houle, a nice wacky-scientist kind of guy, who ran the SCRABBLE Brand Crossword Game Players Division. I wrote some stories for their newspaper; I visited some official SCRABBLE clubs and, at Houle's suggestion, entered a sanctioned SCRABBLE tournament in Connecticut.

It was the first time in my life—but far from the last—that a number of SCRABBLE tournament players greeted me with a blend of suspicion and contempt. I had not done myself any favors in my presentation. For openers, I was wearing a jacket and tie, whereas the players were dressed somewhere between casual and sloppy. Most seemed serious, studious, and humorless. Worse, I was woefully unprepared. I'd barely glanced at the rules, had no idea of the insider's list of key words, and did not give strategy a thought beyond finding a word on my rack and laying it on the board. Even though I'd been placed in the Novice Division, I was destroyed and humiliated in the first three games. My opponents didn't seem to be having much fun either, despite their lopsided victories. At the end of the third game, the pleasant woman in her fifties who had just vanquished me leaned across the table. "Don't take this the wrong way," she said, "but you're in way over your head."

I immediately went over to Jim Houle, who, though not playing, had accompanied me. We agreed that my time would be better spent roaming the playing floor to observe some games and moves. I'd also have lunch and dinner with the players to be better understand both them and SCRABBLE's appeal. In addition, I'd study some of the various written materials around the tournament, including newsletters, word lists, and flyers for upcoming tournaments and more.

By the end of my first tournament weekend, I'd reached three critical realizations. First, there was obviously a lot more to the SCRABBLE subculture than I'd ever realized. Secondly, there was a lot more subtlety to the tournament game than to the living room version. Third, for thousands of people throughout North America, SCRABBLE was far more than a game. It was both a consuming passion and a significant part of their identity.

So it became my job—a mission, ultimately—to recognize this curious passion and tell the story to the rest of the world.

3

HOW A WORD GETS INTO
THE DICTIONARY

PERHAPS THE MOST DOMINANT TOPIC OF conversation throughout my career has been the dictionary. This includes what words are admitted, what words are deleted, how often the dictionary is updated, and the difference between the "American" and the "British" dictionaries. How words get into your everyday desk dictionary is similar to how they find their way into SCRABBLE, so much of the discussion that follows applies to both.

The NSA routinely received calls from indignant SCRABBLE players, many in disbelief that an entry in the *Official SCRABBLE Players Dictionary* is, in fact, a real word. These were mostly living room players as opposed to tournament players. The latter are so used to seeing crazy stuff pop up on an opponent's board that nothing really surprises them, and many have a more-the-merrier attitude when it comes to admissible words.

The aggrieved tend to be longtime casual players, who will frequently cite "the King's English" as their guideline for what words are real and what words are not. The phrase I've probably invoked most often with them over the years is "With all due respect, just because you never heard of it does not mean it's not a real word." I, like my colleagues at Merriam-Webster, believe that the language is a living, breathing entity and that words, meaning, and even grammatical usage are going to change over the course of time. As well they should. Otherwise, we'd all be walking around talking like characters from *Beowulf.*

Chief among the complaints are onomatopoetic words. Examples include MM, HM, HMM, WHOOSH, BRR, BRRR, and the like. These drive people crazy, despite the fact that they tend to be extremely playable and valuable words. I guess there are fewer Ogden Nash fans out there than I'd anticipated.

Another irksome category for word complaints is foreign words. The general rule of thumb is this: if there is no English equivalent, the word finds its way into our everyday language, then onto the pages of the dictionary. There are numerous examples, among them TACO, ADIOS, CIAO (and its alternative spelling JIAO), SI, AMIGO, and CROISSANT. When I explain this criterion, it tends to mollify most complaints. And let's face it. As the world gets smaller because of advances in technology and communication, this phenomenon is going to happen more, not less. This is especially relevant in regard to the Hispanification of the American culture and to the collision course the United States is on with the Middle East. Heck, twenty-five years ago most Americans had never even heard of Cinco de Mayo or a burka—let alone jihad.

Foreign currency tends to annoy people the most. XU, for example, is a monetary unit of South Vietnam and an extremely valuable SCRABBLE word. (For some reason, it does not take an s.)

A ZAIRE is a monetary unit of the former country of the same name. (No, I have no idea why there was such a lack of creativity in Zaire's Treasury Department.) A frustrated SCRABBLE player—a retired schoolteacher—had had enough when she called the NSA to complain about the word. "I dare you," she sputtered, "use the word in a sentence."

I thought for a moment. "How about a zaire for your thoughts?" I suggested. She hung up on me.

Later, I told my NSA friend top tournament veteran Robert Kahn about the encounter. He laughed and said, "Be thankful she didn't confront you about the word REI."

"How come?" I knew the word, of course, but never knew the meaning.

"It's probably the most indefensible word in the game," he said. "Look it up."

I did. REI is "an erroneous English form for a former Portuguese coin." Yeah, he has a point.

This episode brings up the question: How exactly does a word find its way into the dictionary, and where do the words come from? I'll answer the second part first. New words simply arise from the culture, as they have since the beginning of time, from many different corridors.

Some new entries are foreign words being assimilated into English. Technology, recently more than ever, has contributed numerous terms and will continue to do so. Examples include EMAIL, BYTE, WEBMAIL, SPAM, and BITMAP.

As hip-hop culture goes mainstream, it too will provide words and new meanings for existing words. PHAT has been acceptable for some time, and CHILLAX became acceptable in 2014. Other acceptable slang words include AWOL, MOOLAH, YO, and COZ.

Who finds these words, and how is it decided they are worthy of inclusion? The first round in the process is an activity called "reading and marking," and it involves all of the editors at Merriam-Webster.

Visit the desk of one of those editors on any given day and you'll find piles of publications, e-mails, and research covering every aspect of language and society. For example, a reading pile might include such diverse sources as *People* magazine, the *Congressional Record*, a scientific journal, the *National Enquirer*, *TV Guide*, *The New Yorker*, *Yankee* magazine, an educational quarterly, and the like. The task is simple: to read in search of good examples of words used in context. And what are the editors looking for? Most obviously, examples of new words, but also old words being used in new ways, variant spellings, capitalization, inflected forms, and evidence for where the words show up—whether it be in glossy weekly magazines, the *New York Times*, scholarly journals, or even a comic strip. When editors find good examples (also called "citations"), they mark them and send them to a data-entry group that enters them into the citation database. And when the editors have enough citations for a new word, it becomes eligible for admission into the next edition. This is a simplification of the process, believe me, but that is fundamentally how it works. For perspective, know that the Merriam-Webster citation file has citations dating back as far as the 1890s—more than sixteen million of them.

While this process has served us well, it is not immune to changing times—specifically technology and social media. So I asked my colleagues at Merriam-Webster if Facebook, Twitter, YouTube, and the like will streamline the inclusion process in terms of both speed of acceptance and volume of words. Is it possible that new media staples such as LOL, WTF, and BTW will ultimately be viewed as actual "words" and find their way onto a SCRABBLE board?

John Morse, president of Merriam-Webster, was the first to weigh in on the subject. "My initial comment is that the term 'social media' takes in a lot of different kinds of communications. For example, in the physical world, all evidence of language use is noteworthy, but an example of a word taken from the front page of the *New York Times* is going to be more significant than an example taken from a family photograph album. And I think the same applies with social media." Hence the question becomes: How does a "new" word on someone's Facebook page rate in significance compared to one in a Twitter post from, say, the Associated Press? Only time—and future technology—will tell.

Morse agrees that the new-word inclusion process is speeding up. "I would say that the process has already speeded up significantly, and yes, that has happened because of the Web. My sense is that twenty years ago, the shortest lag (with a few notable exceptions) was around ten years, and a typical lag might be closer to twenty. And now, many words are getting in with a lag of five to ten, and sometimes faster than that." He goes on to say, "I do think the overall observation is correct: words establish themselves in the language faster, and we detect that sooner than before. And that happens because of the existence of the Web."

Stephen Perrault, Merriam-Webster's director of defining— now there's a great job title—says, "While we look to digital sources for evidence that we use as the basis for dictionary entries, we don't at this point gather a lot of citations directly from social media." So it appears that while social media will be increasingly a factor in determining dictionary inclusion, evidence from mainstream professionally written and edited sources still prevails.

That said, Perrault reminds us, "I'll note 'the dictionary' itself is now increasingly thought of as an online database rather than (or in addition to) a printed book, and that plays a role in speeding up the process as well."

For some reason, this topic reminds me of the overused quote attributed to Andy Warhol, that in the future "everyone will be famous for fifteen minutes." While we should probably take the statement at face value, there are some who feel the late Pop artist was a media visionary. They make the argument that he meant that one day there would be so much media that there would not be enough celebrities to go around. So, over the years, we have had to elevate the likes of 1994's O. J. Simpson houseguest Kato Kaelin and today's Kim Kardashian to take the place of, perhaps, Walter Cronkite and Grace Kelly. Will the demands of social media become so immediate and deep that there will not be enough new words to go around? I guess we'll see.

As I write this, I am personally involved in this process, following a proposed new definition of the word CATFISH. Here's how it started.

In 2010, two friends and collaborators, Henry Joost and Ariel Schulman, directed a documentary film entitled *Catfish*. It made its debut at the Sundance Film Festival to both wild acclaim and controversy. *Catfish* is a true story that documents the Internet love story of Yaniv "Nev" Schulman, Ariel's brother, as he virtually meets, gets to know, and falls in love with a young woman he randomly met online. When Nev and the filmmakers decided to pay a surprise visit to the young woman, they found out she was not who she pretended to be. To begin with, she was married and perhaps twenty years older than her online persona.

The woman's husband actually inspired the film's title. When told of his wife's deception, he shared an anecdote about a curious practice in the fishing industry. It seems that in the old days cod had a tendency to get sluggish and mushy when being shipped from Alaska to China in large vats. Someone had the idea of throwing catfish into the mix to keep things vibrant and interesting. Hence he depicts his wife similarly, saying with a shrug, "There are those people who are catfish in life."

Fueled by both the Internet and traditional media, CATFISH became a pop culture term in a matter of months. The very first examples of a new meaning for the word were showing up. As a noun, a CATFISH was now an individual who pretended to be someone he or she was not on the Internet. As a verb, one could now get CATFISHED or deceived by an individual with a bogus identity.

Below are a few sample excepts from the citation file at Merriam-Webster that traces the trail of its usage to the ultimate decision to admit CATFISH's new meaning into the dictionary:

After the film's debut, a new definition emerged: "someone who pretends to be someone they're not using Facebook or other social media to create false identities, particularly to pursue online romances."

BOSTON GLOBE, January 27, 2013

Criminal Minds star Thomas Gibson was duped two years ago by a stranger he met online, even sending her a steamy hot tub video. The 51-year-old actor . . . exchanged explicit photos and videos with the North Dakota woman before he discovered he was being catfished and cut off all contact.

TMZ Australia, August 21, 2013

On their new MTV show *Catfish*, Nev Schulman and Max Joseph help people in online relationships discover if they're being duped. . . . After the Manti Te'o hoax . . . "catfish" became part of the national lexicon.

PEOPLE, February 11, 2013

So now you know how a word gets into the dictionary. It happens rarely, but over the years a handful of words have been *removed* from the *Official SCRABBLE Players Dictionary*, or *OSPD*. I'm not talking about the "word purge" of allegedly offensive entries mentioned earlier but about random words that, upon review, were deemed inadmissible by the editors at Merriam-Webster. One that tournament SCRABBLE players miss a lot is KEV, a noun meaning, according to the second edition of the *OSPD*, "a unit of energy." This was a handy word, allowing players to score well with the K and V while eliminating those cumbersome letters in favor of some more bingo-prone. ("Bingo" is an insider's term for a play using all seven tiles.) However, it was ultimately decided that KEV was not a word but rather an abbreviation. Bummer.

Another handy word removed from the *OSPD* in later editions was DA. It is an Italian preposition meaning "from," as in the name of the explorer Vasco da Gama. However, it was eventually decided that DA was *too* Italian, or perhaps *only* Italian. After further consideration, Merriam-Webster decided it was *ciao* for

DA. But DA was not DOA for long. It resurfaced in the fifth edition in 2014, now defined as a term of endearment.

One of my favorites is the word STETSON. It appeared in the original *OSPD*, defined as a "broad-brimmed hat." However, STETSON was gone by the second edition, published in 1990. It had been determined by Merriam-Webster—and perhaps by attorneys from the hat company—that STETSON was a trademarked name, and hence properly capitalized and hence not playable according to Rule 8 of the SCRABBLE game. Yet it appears again today in the list of acceptable words for tournament play. What happened?

STETSON was a case of diverging opinions from the two authorities who compile and select words for the *OSPD* and its companion volume, the *Official Tournament and Club Word List*, or *OWL*. The first group, of course, is the editorial staff at Merriam-Webster. The second is the official Dictionary Committee of, until 2013, the National SCRABBLE Association and currently NASPA, the NSA's successor, the North American SCRABBLE Players Association. This is a group of hardcore word enthusiasts with strong opinions and the knowledge to back them up. As head of the NSA, I was automatically a member of the Dictionary Committee. I can say with certainty I did not make a single contribution to the Dictionary Committee in twenty-five years. I wouldn't have dared.

Just as civilians disagree about what words are good in SCRABBLE, the pros do as well. The NSA Dictionary Committee argued that STETSON falls into the same category as ASPIRIN or MIMEOGRAPH—brand names that culturally are frequently used as generic words. "Some words meet our criteria, but not Merriam-Webster's," notes former NASPA Dictionary Committee chairman Jim Pate. Remember, most tournament SCRABBLE players are looking for as many words to play as possible. Merriam-Webster, on the other hand, has to be mindful of the legal status of words. If a registered trademark is in effect, then the trademark status must be recognized and the word must be capitalized and hence falls prey to Rule 8.

However, with the creation and publishing of the *OWL* in 1998, a middle ground was reached. Merriam-Webster agreed, albeit reluctantly, to accommodate the NSA Dictionary Committee. Here are some *OWL* words:

AQUALUNG	LATINA
BENADRYL	LEVIS
BIRO	LUCITE
BRILLO	LYCRA
BUDDHA	MAILGRAM
CATHOLICS	MASONITE
CROCKPOT	NONGLARES
DACRON	ORLON
DUMPSTER	POPSICLE
EMMY	PYREX
ENUF	SORTA
FORMICA	TEFLON
FRISBEE	TOFUTTI
JACUZZI	TRES
JELLO	VASELINE
JETWAY	VELCRO
KEWPIE	WIMMIN
KLEENEX	ZLOTIES

Clearly, many of these are proper-noun product names. Yet the case can be made—and was—that they've become so integrated into everyday language that they belong on a SCRABBLE board.

The back-and-forth word forays in both general dictionaries and the *Official SCRABBLE Players Dictionary* serve to remind us that the English language is a growing, evolving, occasionally contracting entity in regard to both meanings and usage. Traditionalists who bemoan the deterioration of "the King's English" would be well advised to rethink their criteria.

4

WASH OUR MOUTHS
OUT WITH SOAP

N THE EARLY 1990S, TWO WOMEN were playing SCRABBLE in suburban Washington, DC. At one point in the game, a word was challenged. The players decided to settle the dispute by checking the *Official SCRABBLE Players Dictionary, Second Edition*. However, in skimming the pages, the women stumbled across the word KIKE. Understandably, they were appalled. And, in a you-can't-make-this-stuff-up scenario, one of the two women was a Holocaust survivor.

The pair proceeded to scour the book. To their horror and disappointment, they found not only every possible slur against Jews (JEW as a verb, KIKE, HEBE, YID) but those against blacks, Hispanics, Catholics, gays, and any other group one could name.

By the end of this exercise, the women were on a mission. They were going to have these words removed from SCRABBLE. Their first step was to get in touch with Hasbro, the game's maker.

I'm not sure whom they talked to that first time, but they were essentially rebuffed by the simple but correct explanation that any word in the dictionary that is not a proper noun is acceptable in SCRABBLE play. After all, lexicographers cannot pretend a word doesn't exist just because someone doesn't like it. Also, however noble the intention, it's naïve to assume that if a word is removed from any dictionary, it's going to disappear from the language and conversation.

The dismissal from a Hasbro rep only inflamed the women further. So they took their case to the Anti-Defamation League (ADL), the powerful and effective organization dedicated to fighting anti-Semitism. As one might imagine, the group was all over the situation.

The ADL quickly fired off a letter to Alan Hassenfeld, chairman and CEO of Hasbro at the time, accusing the company of "playing games with hate." Hassenfeld, whose family was active in Jewish charities and causes, was in a tough spot, but he knew he had to act quickly. So he replied that Hasbro would remove all offensive words from the *OSPD* as soon as possible.

Because I was the person in the middle between Hasbro, the media, the dictionary publisher, and the players, the job fell to me and the NSA staff to both orchestrate this process and communicate progress to all those entities. The initial phone call went something like this.

"John, we need you to take all the offensive words out of the SCRABBLE dictionary."

"Which ones?" I asked, not joking.

"You know," the Hasbro exec continued, "all the usual curse words, body parts, racial and religious slurs, that kind of stuff."

He made it sound so simple. But I knew better. For openers, the mid-1990s was perhaps the zenith of the political correctness movement, when, it could be argued, people sometimes went overboard in trying to do or say the correct thing.

My favorite example of this was the case in January 1999 of a Washington, DC, political aide, David Howard, who was quoted in the press as saying something about the need to be more "niggardly" in the management of certain city funds. NIGGARDLY, of course, is an old English word, admittedly obscure, defined as "grudgingly mean about spending."

However, there was a rush to judgment because the word *sounded* like what we refer to as "the N-word." In fact, it seemed the guy was having his resignation accepted before anyone could even open a dictionary. And when someone finally did, it was too late. Attempts to explain the real meaning were cumbersome and ineffective, as people were already too agitated. The rationale then seemed to me to waver to this: the guy should have lost his job for *bad judgment*—selecting a word that sounded too much like an offensive term. Finally, reason prevailed; he was rehired by the mayor's office.

So, accompanied by my NSA colleague Joe Edley, I began the dubious quest to find every despicable word in the English language to appease the Hasbro attorneys, the Anti-Defamation League, and anyone else who thought or hoped a word was going to disappear from use and the language simply by being removed from a game-related dictionary. We were aware as we began that this task was a bizarre blend of dangerous, silly, pointless, and futile. Worse, for me, was that it pitted my job requirements against my strong personal belief in free speech. Ah, the classic American dilemma, choosing between one's job and the Constitution.

Some of the considerations were complicated. For example, the words PANSY, CHICK, DICK, FAGGOT, BITCH, HOMO, and the like are all hateful slurs, but they all have alternative, harmless meanings. So these words survived the cut with the offensive definition deleted.

The word MOTHERFUCKER was discussed, but was not part of the assignment because the *Official SCRABBLE Players Dictionary* only goes up to eight-letter words. (Over 90 percent of all SCRABBLE plays are eight letters or fewer.) But the conversation about the word reminded us of a famous story that came out of a Tennessee SCRABBLE club back in the 1980s.

As the story went, a young man in his thirties was beginning a game against woman in her eighties. His absolute best opening play was the word SHITTY. He stared at the word on his rack, then at the sweet face and carefully coiffed white hair of his opponent. He agonized. He looked back at her face, back at his rack. He just couldn't play the word. Instead, the young man made a much safer play for far fewer points. But he had no doubt he'd done the right thing. Across the board, the older woman studied his opening play for a minute or so. Then she threw down the word FUCKERS for 80-something points, shrugged, and happily wrote down her score.

This story gets to one of the key points of this entire issue. In SCRABBLE, words are simply game pieces. Expert players often know thousands of words for which they do not know—nor are they required to know—the meaning. As both *Word Freak* author Stefan Fatsis and Will Shortz, *New York Times* crossword puzzle editor, have stated to me: in SCRABBLE, meanings are meaningless.

Obviously, this situation flies in the face of all cultural and linguistic standards. We learn early in life that all words do in fact have meaning and, at times, the attendant power. Words are—or at least should be—chosen with care for reasons of emphasis, sensitivity, clarity, and desired impact. So the concept of them being "meaningless" is both disconcerting and anti-intuitive, even just for the sake of playing a game.

But I digress. Our search continued. In addition to all the naughty words we could think of, we asked our colleagues at Merriam-Webster, the country's foremost lexicographers, to send us a list of every word that had a designation in their files as vulgar, profane, racist, a religious or ethnic slur, and the like. It goes without saying, the editors at Merriam-Webster were appalled that we were even doing this.

Some of their words were amusing. Did you know that PAPIST (a Roman Catholic) and JESUIT (a scheming person) are considered religious slurs? I can't say I've seen either used that way in my lifetime, perhaps scrawled somewhere on a church wall by a hate-filled graffiti artist. However, both words were used in a derogatory manner against Roman Catholics—depicting them as enemies of the Church of England—as far back as the early sixteenth century.

There were others, equally absurd or obscure. In all, we came up with about 175 allegedly offensive candidates. We submitted them to Hasbro for review. Our memo covered both our collective asses and two fundamental points: the list was by nature incomplete, and offensiveness is nothing if not subjective. It's like humor; one person's double entendre is another person's banana peel.

Later, a senior Hasbro Games division executive tried to grandstand at a meeting, proudly announcing we had overlooked the word TUP. When asked its meaning, he preened, "It means to have sex with a sheep."

I waited a minute for the room to absorb this information. I finally spoke. "Yes, I know the word. It means for a *ram* to have sex with a ewe, not a couple of drunken farm boys. It's a veterinary term."

The Offensive-Word story went viral, and within a week the story broke nationally in the publishing column in the *New York Daily News* written by veteran journalist Paul Colford. I was just leaving an associate's office at MTV Networks, where I was working on a writing project, when his assistant shoved a handful of those pink message slips at me. They read: John, call NBC News; John, the *Wall Street Journal* is trying to make a deadline, call ASAP; John, can you do an interview for *CNN* for the 6 o'clock news; John, the *Miami Herald* style section editor needs a photo-call immediately; and whatever you do, John, please call your office *FIRST*—they are swamped with more calls.

After a couple of conference calls, Merriam-Webster, Hasbro, and I agreed that I would be the only official spokesperson on the issue. It had also been decided—not by me—that I would not be allowed to disclose any specific word that was going to be eliminated from SCRABBLE. You can imagine how that went over with journalists.

As a writer myself, I understood the idiocy and frustration of it all for them. Here was an explosive story on any number of levels, yet the press was not given access to the newly created offensive-word list. So they and I were reduced to a silly dance along the lines of "Okay, Mr. Williams. How about I say a word and you can tell me whether or not it will be banned from SCRABBLE. Can you at least do that?"

So they wrote the stories anyway—scores of them—guessing at the banned words or suggesting readers simply use their imaginations.

Personally, the worst part of this experience was that somehow it became assumed that I was not only the individual who decided to remove "offensive" words from SCRABBLE play, but also the one in charge of selecting those words. That's when the fecal matter really hit the fan.

I began to receive letters and phone calls from all over the world.

- A man from Wales insisted that the word WELSH be removed because it had the same connotation as JEW used as a verb.

- In the same vein, I received an impassioned letter from a gentleman who identified himself as the official United Nations delegate representing the 1.1 million Romani (Gypsies) in North America. He asked that the word GYP (to swindle)—similar in meaning to JEW and WELSH—be removed as it was a slur against his constituents. His letter was accompanied by several pages of data, which theoretically proved Romani were the most maligned race in the world in regards to ethnic prejudice. Who knew?

- An Irishman lobbied for removal of the word PADDY-WAGON, as its origin was something like "a small truck filled with drunken Irishmen." Of course, PADDYWAGON wasn't even in the SCRABBLE dictionary because it was more than eight letters.

- An ardent feminist demanded that the word HISTORY be removed as it was blatantly sexist. Happily, the word HERSTORY was added to the SCRABBLE dictionary a few years later. OURSTORY perhaps waits in the wings for future admission.

- A pacifist wrote, "I consider WAR and GUN to be the two most dangerous words in the English language and respectfully request they be considered for deletion." Being a pacifist, he did not demand, insist, or threaten.
- Finally, in the mail came this. "I deplore what you are doing, Mr. Williams. I will find you and rectify this injustice." We called postal authorities and the FBI on that one. Remarkably, the sender had left a legitimate return address on the letter. Now that's commitment.

This entire exercise proved what I had said from the initial conversation, when I was charged with removing the offensive words from the SCRABBLE dictionary. Which ones?

When the dust finally settled on all this, a couple of things happened. The *Official SCRABBLE Players Dictionary* was revised as the Third Edition in 1995 with approximately 175 words removed. However, in a compromise enacted by the NSA, all words remained allowable in official club and tournament play in the United States and Canada. This was the genesis of the *OWL*, which had all the words but, as per the agreement with Hasbro, no definitions. It was available only to members of the National SCRABBLE Association. We, after all, were trained word professionals and would not let them fall into the wrong hands.

For educational purposes only, I've included the notorious word list in the appendix. I suspect you'll be turning there now.

At the end of it all, only one tournament player I know of resigned from the NSA. He returned about a decade later. He assured me, after one day back at the National SCRABBLE Championship, that it was "as gloriously crazy as ever." He was right. You can screw around with the words, but the people will prevail.

5

HOW I BECAME A PLAYER

I T BECAME CLEAR TO ME THAT sooner or later I had to become a credible tournament player if I was to do my job well and effectively. However, I was a couple of years into being executive director of the NSA before I made a real commitment. I knew there would be a lot of time and study involved, not to mention the risk of looking stupid to a large number of people. Hence my reluctance.

Fortunately, I had Joe Edley as a teacher. Joe was, until 2011, the only person to win the National SCRABBLE Championship (NSC) three times. New Zealander Nigel Richards has since won the event a staggering five times, as well as the World SCRABBLE Championship (WSC) three times. He's now considered the greatest to have ever played the game—with no end in sight. Dave Wiegand, a resident of Portland, Oregon, has won the NSC twice and is always a threat to duplicate Joe's effort.

Remarkably, Joe accomplished this in three different decades: 1980, 1992, and 2000. One of the best tournament players in history, he is famous for his Zen-like mental approach to competition, which many opponents found both irritating and distracting. His tai chi exercises between rounds were legendary. One could often see Joe in the corner of a huge ballroom, silently morphing into meditative poses. Comical to many, it worked for him.

Joe is a masterful teacher. He has the patience of someone who has memorized 125,000 or so words and the passion of one who believes the world would be a better place if everyone played more SCRABBLE. A mathematician by education, Joe also has a very logical, systematic, and unemotional approach to any task. So the entire exercise was like being taught by Mr. Spock from *Star Trek*.

The cornerstone of our lessons was what is called an "open game," where we would see each other's racks and discuss the various options of each move. Among other skills learned in this technique is what players call "rack management," which means learning the thought process and steps in making a good SCRABBLE move. Among the considerations are these:

- Check out all the possible places on the board for a play. This is what we call "board vision." Start by checking all the bonus squares, or "hot spots."
- Look at those spots from both an offensive and defensive point of view. It's very often a balance. You want to score as many points as possible, but if it sets up your opponent for a big play it may not be worth it. And always check to see if there's already a dangerous opening for your opponent; it may make sense to block it with even a modest-scoring word.
- Remember, the best play is not always the most points

(this tends to be a huge flaw in many commercial SCRABBLE apps). Unless you're laying down a 7-letter play (bingo), a good SCRABBLE move is comprised of two parts: what you put on the board to score and what you leave yourself to work with on your rack. Think about it. If you make a high-scoring play but leave yourself with v, u, u, you've pretty much guaranteed your next three plays are not going to be favorable.

For a year Joe and I tried to play at least one open game almost every day. Early on, I would also have for reference the NSA's "secret word list." Compiled by expert player Mike Baron, this is a compendium of about 1,500 of the most valuable words every tournament player should know. It includes all two-letter words and three-letter words, common words using the power tiles j, q, x, and z, the vowel-dump list for a rack with too many vowels, and the q-without-u words. Using this sheet of words allowed me to both learn them and realize their strategic importance. In fact, learning these words was the first thing the NSA encouraged anyone wanting to become a better player to do.

It was twenty years ago, but I still have some random memories of those lessons. I'm sure Joe and I played at least three hundred games before I won a single match, and even then, I definitely had the better tiles. But I do remember the first time I defeated Joe. Obviously, I was overjoyed. Even better, Joe was extremely gracious. He was absolutely delighted for me. Of course, in my naïveté, I was sure this was a milestone and things would begin to even out between us, albeit incrementally. Joe, on the other hand, most certainly knew we could go another fifty or more games before I won again. He was right.

Two early plays I recall were seven-letter moves, both plurals. One was GUNITES. I'd seen the word around here and there and thought it was some sort of material used in the construction of swimming pools. That turned out to be true, but it also turned out that the word wasn't playable because it was a trademark and therefore capitalized; since then it's become acceptable. Another was FUNGOES, which I knew from baseball (a type of hit or a special bat used in practice). This word was good, and even better, Joe challenged it! I still lost.

So our practice games were enormously helpful, and I did in fact slowly progress. The games got incrementally closer. My strategy and board vision improved. And I was learning the words.

Everyone has his or her own way to memorize. Like Joe, I created my own flash cards. Remember, this was before all the numerous and refined studying techniques now available online or via customized software.

My methodology was a highly personal and random blend of mnemonics and word association. Here are some examples:

- I could never remember early on which was acceptable, PIA or MIA, so I did an index card that said PIA GOOD, MIA is *M*issing *I*n *A*ction. Hey, don't judge me; it worked.
- Another card was to learn the "back hooks" for the word ox—single letters that could be added to make a playable word. This one read: *OY!! OX TAKES AN O & Y (OXO, OXY)* Again, this worked for me.
- Other times, I'd just stack them visually:

TIKI
TIPI
TITI

In all, I probably created two hundred flash cards. Often, during a game, I was able to visualize myself actually writing the card out, which was enormously helpful.

Eventually, I decided to test the state of my fledgling tournament game. What better place than the belly of the beast—the notorious New York City SCRABBLE Club.

There were numerous stories about the club in regard to both the level of play and the atmosphere. The skill level was high, with numerous top-ranked experts. They regularly included Joel Sherman, Joe Edley, Ron Tiekert, Robert Felt, Ed Halper, Rita Norr, Rose Kreiswirth, Richie Lund, Lynne Cushman, and Paul Avrin. The atmosphere, depending on the night, ranged from hospitable to hostile. Hey, this was New York.

I had no illusions about this foray for my tune-up experience before my first tournament. I was achingly self-conscious about both my reception and my performance at the board. I knew many New York SCRABBLE players were contemptuous of the National SCRABBLE Association and authority in general, and this added unwanted pressure.

I played three games that night. I was completely destroyed in one by a low-rated intermediate player. I held my own in a close match with another player of the same caliber. However, the third game was something special.

Cruelly, I'd been matched up with one of the top players in the city. I'm not sure how this happened, but it did. It was clear from the onset that he was not taking me—or our game—seriously. Who could blame him? This first clue was that he didn't even bother to track tiles. (Tournament players have a preprinted sheet of the 100 game tiles and can check them off as they're played, so as the game progresses they have a better sense of what letters are available.) The second clue was that he played the complete game upside down, not even bothering to turn the board to himself for a better look.

The good tiles were spilt fairly equally between us, and it ended up being a close game, with one bingo each. As the bag became emptier, I realized that the Q had not been played. I then scanned the board and realized that three of the four U's had been expended in earlier plays. Since my opponent was not tracking tiles, it occurred to me that he hadn't seen this situation developing.

As we reached the final turns, I had drawn the final U and he had drawn the Q. All of a sudden, he started to pay serious attention. But it was too late. The board had been shut down for a Q-play for him. I ended up winning the game by a couple of points because he had to "eat the Q" for a costly 20 points at the end. It's only fair to point out that this game took place well before QAT became acceptable, let alone QI. But I'll take it.

Buoyed by my practice games at the New York City club, I was ready for my first tournament, the Long Island Championship. It was held in Port Jefferson, New York, on St. Patrick's weekend in 1991. There were about fifty players in three divisions for a ten-game event. I was in the Novice Division.

As in many aspects of my life, my goal was not necessarily to excel but simply to not embarrass myself. Had I been able to enter this event in disguise with an alternative identity, that would have been fine with me.

I attended an opening reception and talked mostly about
SCRABBLE and words. Of course, everyone knew who I was.
Many wished me luck and welcomed me to the fold. Others
peppered me with questions and complaints about the NSA—
missing newsletters, high dues, low prize money, and the like.
It helped give me perspective on Joe Edley's tournament experiences in the two-plus decades he was serving as NSA's director
of clubs and tournaments.

Some people complained that Joe had some sort of advantage
working at the NSA and being a competitive player at the same
time. Chief among these was Bronx lawyer Ed Halper, a top
player and club director. Every year when he renewed his NSA
membership he'd write "FIRE EDLEY" on the check. But think
about it. Not only was everyone gunning for Edley, but at every
tournament his concentration would be broken between rounds
with garden-variety questions about the SCRABBLE organization. No wonder Joe retreated into frequent tai chi trances!

In reality, without Joe Edley there is no way the National
SCRABBLE Association could have achieved everything it
did. Joe handled an enormous workload with ease and grace
and helped the NSA forge its belief in the sanctity of the game.
Among Joe's contributions:

- Edited and wrote much of the *SCRABBLE News*
- Scheduled two hundred SCRABBLE tournaments a year
- Administered and scored the NSA Club Director's
  Tests
- Handled player disputes
- Oversaw day-to-day participation in the *OSPD*
- Fielded numerous phone calls and correspondence

- ■ Helped organize and direct National, World, and School SCRABBLE events
- ■ Maintained the official NSA Ratings System
- ■ Contributed heavily to the creation of NSA membership materials
- ■ Created numerous puzzles and word quizzes
- ■ Helped strategize NSA growth
- ■ Interacted with SCRABBLE manufacturers on product development, testing, and marketing
- ■ Gave numerous lectures and made other appearances

The SCRABBLE tournament scene and I personally owe Joe Edley an enormous amount of gratitude for his contributions to the game.

Now, back to my first official SCRABBLE tournament. It was around 8:00 p.m. on a Friday when I sat down across from my first opponent, a guy in his forties whom I'd never met. We wished each other luck, shook hands, and drew tiles to see who went first. He did, as he chose a tile closer to A. Inside, I sighed a bit. I'd learned that whoever goes first in a SCRABBLE match statistically has a 55 percent chance of winning.

Decades later, I couldn't tell you what my first rack was. But I remember my opponent's first play. He laid down COWY. Surprisingly, in both the course of my everyday life and in my studying obscure words for the game, I'd never seen that word. Ever. Not in a book. Not on the word lists I'd studied.

Complicating this was the fact that I'd promised myself that in this tournament, I was going to challenge any word I did not know. Yet here, in the very first play of my tournament career, I was second-guessing myself. My opponent had played COWY with such nonchalance and confidence, it had me rattled. I asked myself which was worse: being duped by a phony in the first play of my first tournament or challenging a word that might have been routine even in the Novice Division.

Ultimately, I decided not to challenge. And it was a good thing. cowy was indeed acceptable. cowy means "suggestive of a cow." Happily, I went on to win that game. Twenty years later, however, I've still never heard or seen the word used even once outside of SCRABBLE.

The whole issue of playing phonies is both nuanced and controversial. Living room players—an arguably dismissive term tournament players use—generally disapprove of playing phony words. That quite possibly is the genesis of the needing-to-know-the-definition house rule many people believe to be official. It's not.

I played two more games that first night and ended up 3–0! That performance was beyond my expectations, and it propelled me into a blend of confidence and looseness I'd rarely experienced in any competition. Over the years, I'd heard athletes and SCRABBLE experts like talk about being "in the zone." I was definitely there. It was almost as if I were channeling someone else's ability and someone else's luck. I cannot remember many specifics of that evening, but it's a safe bet I was getting my share of valuable tiles. How else could I have done that?

I'd attended the tournament with my friend Rob Buchanan, a veteran journalist. A very good casual player himself, Rob had entered the competition thinking there might be a story there. He lived across the street from me, and we played many practice matches together. However, he hadn't really studied any word lists, so he was at a disadvantage even in the Novice Division.

The evening had not treated Rob as well. I recall he was 0–3 and not happy about it. A trip to the hotel bar seemed in order. After a couple of drinks, Rob and I decided to do what most tournament players do after a long day of competition: play more SCRABBLE. So we headed back to my room to break out the board.

At the bar, Rob and I had engaged in some spirited trash-talking. In reality, our SCRABBLE abilities were pretty close. So Rob chided me about being lucky, having inferior opponents to his, that sort of thing. Thus by the time we started play, our after-hours match had taken on the good-natured intensity of a showdown.

We poured an unnecessary third drink as we opened the board. A potential wager was discussed, then dismissed. Bragging rights would do. We drew to go first. In keeping with the evening's vibe, I selected an A.

Then I drew my seven tiles, arranged them on my rack, and stared in disbelief. There before me was the word ANCHOVY.

Talk about being in the zone. I stared at the word for another couple of seconds. Then I laid it down on the board. "Anchovy," I announced with poorly disguised glee, "94 points."

Rob stared silently at the board. He then turned his gaze to me as he stood and pushed his chair back. "Fuck you," he said, grinning and shaking his head. Rob went on to finish 5–5, a respectable performance for anyone's first tournament. We are still friends and neighbors, but we don't play SCRABBLE together anymore.

For the most part, the tournament continued the way it had started. I finally lost an afternoon game to a delightful woman named Stacia Camp, who showed me afterward how I could have—*should have*—won our match. By the end of the day, my record was 6–1 with three games left to play on Sunday morning. I was leading my division.

At this point in the weekend, my performance was starting to attract some attention from everyone, experts included. Players in all divisions were very gracious and supportive. Some suggested I was really an Intermediate Division competitor "playing down" and was a Novice only because it was my first tournament. All I know is that I was damn relieved to have at least shown I knew the game. My instructor, Joe Edley, competing in the Expert Division, was thrilled.

The rest of the tournament was pretty much a blur. I remember finding—and nervously playing—the word IRONIST against a skeptical opponent. It was good. I won another. IRONIST, by the way, means "one who uses irony." Keep an eye out for it on future racks. The common letters make it appear quite often.

I was 8–1 going into the last round, matched against a young woman who was, I believe, 8–1 as well. She was very good and had played in several tournaments. With a victory, I'd win the whole thing. A loss on my part would tie us, and whoever had the bigger point spread in all the games would be the champion.

I remember the game was back and forth with several lead changes. Then we got to the very end. She was ahead by perhaps 40 points with about a dozen tiles left in the bag. I drew well on the next opportunity and ended up with the bingo ENTAILS.

Unfortunately, I scoured the board three times and realized there was no place to play it. SCRABBLE players know this is perhaps the most frustrating situation in the game—a bingo with no place to lay it down. Panicking, I frantically moved the tiles around on my rack looking for another word in this favorable group of tiles.

I'm sure any expert player watching would have immediately seen the other words: ELASTIN, NAILSET, SALIENT, SLAINTE, TENAILS. With the exception of SALIENT, I didn't yet know any of those words. The only one I could come up with was SALTINE.

So I sat and stared at my rack. I was pretty sure that SALTINE was a proper noun, a trademarked cracker name owned by Nabisco or the like. Yet a small part of me reasoned that it could be a generic word for a type of cracker.

The pressure was mounting as I rechecked the clock, rechecked the score, and scanned the placid face of my opponent. Finally, I accepted the fact that I had no choice. In a display of shaky confidence I laid down the word SALTINE.

Now it was her turn to think it over. She wrote the word down on a piece of paper and studied it. Then she looked back and forth at the board as if something might have changed. She had no choice either. If she did not challenge, I would win. Her best chance—a very good one—was that SALTINE was a phony.

It is not. According to the *Official SCRABBLE Players Dictionary*, SALTINE is defined as, duh, "a salted cracker." I won the challenge. I won the game. I won my tournament division with a 9–1 record. I was stunned, euphoric, in disbelief. Oh yeah, I also won $100, which I returned to the prize pool.

Little did I know it would be the highlight of my SCRABBLE tournament career. I should have listened to Mike Baron, who told me the day after the victory, "Consider retiring right now. You could go in the record books with one of the most impressive tournament debuts in history and lifetime winning percentage."

Instead, I made what was probably one of the stupidest moves in SCRABBLE tournament history. It occurred exactly one year later, again at the Long Island SCRABBLE Championship. By virtue of my previous win, I now had a tournament rating of 1554. The NSA rating system was originally based on a variation of the one used in chess. Simply put, it essentially calculates how well you do against other rated players.

The ratings fall into three groups: Novice is 600–1199, Intermediate is 1200–1599, and Expert is 1600+. But as we grew, NSA rules allowed a player to "play up" a division in most tournaments. So in my cluelessness and arrogance, I thought, hey, I'm just 46 points from an official Expert rating. Why not play with the best? How cool, I thought. In just my second SCRABBLE tournament, I was already good enough to compete against the very top players.

This is a cautionary tale, so pay attention. For I was to learn a painful lesson: the difference between almost having an Expert rating and being an expert player.

When I arrived at the tournament, most of the experts treated me with at best a sense of bemusement. They already knew what I did not: I didn't belong in the same room with them. As a rule, experts also don't like lesser competitors "playing up." That's because should an expert by chance lose a game to the weaker opponent, the expert's rating will take a beating. If a 1366 player beats a 1941 player, his or her rating will rise appreciably, and the opposite will happen to the expert.

Well, it became clear they had nothing to worry about with me. I was in for a reality check of the highest order. Going into the final afternoon, my record was 0–10—almost the complete opposite of the previous year. Worse, I imagined myself being perceived by the other players as either a laughingstock or a pathetic figure. The only saving grace is that I come from the hit-over-the-head-with-a-shovel school of learning stuff. I was in familiar territory. I simply sucked it up and went on. Fortunately, I drew good tiles in the last two games and won them both for a 2–10 record, finishing dead last in the Expert Division.

Though technically still eligible, I knew I'd never play in the Expert Division again. My rating had dropped to 1493, which theoretically made me a "high Intermediate." I say theoretically because my bumpy, ragged tournament experiences were far from over.

I was starting to learn a couple of key lessons about the tournament game and environment. For openers, it's important to remember that every time you sit down across from someone, chances are that person is as good as or better than you. That dynamic seldom exists when you compete at home, against friends. For the most part, I'd been a better player than most of the people I'd played. They were very smart people, excellent living room players who played SCRABBLE for, God forbid, fun.

I also learned that playing only periodically in official SCRABBLE tournaments was not the way to do it. There is a "rust factor" that can easily cost you a game or two. It could be the chess clock ticking off your twenty-five minutes, an intimidating opponent, playing six games in a day, sleeping in a strange bed, whatever. So I didn't do myself any favors by playing only one or two tournaments a year; I did a favor for the rest of the competition.

Probably the most resonant lesson from the experience is this: if you don't study, you are not going to get any better. Period. With the exception of my first tournament, I never took studying words very seriously. The reality is you can play twenty-five games a day, and have great strategic skills and board vision—

but if you don't know the words, you'll likely be saddled with the same rating forever.

In retrospect, I'd take that deal right now. As I write this, my rating is 1293, and my last full tournament was in August of 2007. Offering solace, Joe Edley assured me, "Your skills have not diminished. You're probably as good as or better than when you were rated 1554." What's changed, Joe explained, is that the ratings system has been altered slightly and that there are so many better players now in all divisions. My lifetime tournament record is 35–68, a winning percentage of .340. However, in my defense, my scores averaged a respectable 367 points a game. Mercifully, the statistic of the average score *against* me was unavailable.

I still toy with the idea of someday playing in a National SCRABBLE Championship. Despite thirty years of involvement with the game, I was never able to do it because of other obligations at these events. It's the Olympics of SCRABBLE, with the best players in the world in the same room as first-timers. In addition to the competition, it's also a celebration of the glorious game and those who've made it a significant part of their life. Look around the giant ballroom that houses a National SCRABBLE Championship and you'll see a veritable Noah's Ark of humanity. The game draws every single type of person imaginable.

And I have a plan for my return. First I'll play in a couple of local tournaments leading up to, say, the 2015 NSC. If my past performance is any indication, my rating should continue to systematically plummet. Ideally, I'd enter my first National SCRABBLE Championship with a rating between 1136 and 1171. That would put me squarely in the Novice Division. I think I would do really well there, but could I last the thirty-plus rounds in four days?

I've been asked many times, both casually and in interviews, to reveal a few pointers for improving one's SCRABBLE play. I've assembled ten tips to keep in mind that will accomplish just that, and they are available in the appendix at the end of the book. These are taken from the book *Everything SCRABBLE*® by me and three-time National SCRABBLE Champion Joe Edley.

6

MEDIA TIME

AMONG THE MANY RESPONSIBILITIES OF MY SCRABBLE job was media relations. Previously, the task was called "public relations," but apparently that term fell out of favor because it was either too limiting or did not sound important enough. As one of my advertising friends used to tell me, "I can only charge about $1,200 for an idea, but I can get as much as $2,500 for a *concept*!"

One of my early goals was to convince Hasbro executives to make the story or event always about SCRABBLE and never about Hasbro. As a result we never had a single Hasbro banner or sign at any SCRABBLE Championship over two decades— heresy in marketing circles! Yet it paid off. Keeping the perception of SCRABBLE as a generic game made it more palatable to the media and corporate partners. When I called to pitch a SCRABBLE story to a newspaper or television show, I was not calling as a Hasbro exec or from a PR agency. I was calling from the independent National SCRABBLE Association.

And the event was never the "Hasbro" National SCRABBLE Championship.

Chief among our media-related tasks was booking a recently crowned SCRABBLE champion on one of the national morning shows: *Good Morning America, Today,* or *CBS This Morning.* Fortunately, we've been able to arrange numerous appearances over the years on these shows, as well as other outlets such as *Jimmy Kimmel Live!, The Martha Stewart Show,* and CNN, to name just a few.

A media favorite, one of the most colorful and beloved SCRABBLE Champions ever is "G.I. Joel" Sherman of the Bronx. His nickname was derived from his well-known gastrointestinal (GI, get it?) distress, which manifested itself in many forms. Oh, and he had to expectorate frequently.

No one in the SCRABBLE world ever thought twice about these quirks, which would have been questionably tolerated in the outside world. Joel is a great guy, a wonderful ambassador for the game. Hell, some would argue that having personality quirks is almost a prerequisite for a top SCRABBLE expert.

One particular memory resonates. We were backstage at *Today,* and I was prepping Joel for his appearance. We discussed the talking points we wanted to cover. We reviewed highlights and interesting words played. We outlined ways to prevent him from burping during his four minutes with Katie Couric. Just as Joel was about to go onstage, he turned to me and thrust a Styrofoam cup in my direction.

"Here," he said to me, "hold my mucus cup, okay?" I reluctantly grabbed the dubious vessel. A young NBC production assistant looked over to me. "Dude," he said, grinning, "they don't pay you enough."

I'm happy to say that Joel's interview with Katie Couric was flawless, funny, informative, and unassuming. He walked off the set and headed my way. I quickly pushed the mucus cup back in his direction.

The National SCRABBLE Championship was always the most important media outreach the NSA conducted. Started in 1978 by Selchow & Righter, it was held annually or semiannually in major cities all over the country. Over the years, participation ranged from just thirty-two players in 1983 in Chicago (an invitational format) to over eight hundred contestants in New Orleans in 2004.

The National SCRABBLE Association officially took over organizing and promoting the NSC in 1988. Over the years, this involved putting together a complex blueprint for an event. The process always began with selecting a host city in a major market. There were specific criteria for selection:

■ Tourism appeal for the players' families and contestants themselves in off-hours
■ Reasonably easy to get to from anywhere
■ A selection of hotels with good rates and many nearby affordable dining options
■ A good media town, i.e., strong daily newspaper, AP office, NPR station, local talk radio, network-affiliate television stations

There were all kinds of logistics as well. We had to hire word judges, a team of computer programmers and data-entry personnel to handle the thousands of rating calculations, division leaders and assistants to handle rulings and player questions, a photographer, an online reporter, and a video team for in-house or Internet telecasts. (Typically, we would get up to six million hits with people watching the play-by-play commentary on our website.) In total, we often assembled a staff of up to thirty-five people to help us run an NSC.

While the National SCRABBLE Championship was seen by its participants as an annual or semiannual celebration of their culture and the ultimate competitive experience, we, of course, also had to tend to the business end. That meant getting national publicity to raise awareness of both the SCRABBLE brand and the glories of the tournament scene. Given some of the players' reluctance to be on television or in the media at all—and their resentment of corporate interference with their beloved game— we often had to do a delicate dance to make that happen. It made for some interesting challenges.

One year, both the sponsor and its New York media relations agency were concerned as we were heading toward the finals because the favorite to win the championship was deemed by them to be "not telegenic." A wonderful young genius, he was painfully shy and, to their thinking, somewhat unkempt. It had also been established by the player himself that—unlike most people—he couldn't have cared less whether he was on television or not.

The stakes were high, as we were already booked for an appearance on *Today* three days after the finals. This kind of "PR hit" could be considered worth over a million dollars—way more than the entire cost of putting on an event like this.

About thirty-six hours before the finals, the media exec took me aside. "Is there a way we can manipulate the scoring or pairings to minimize his chances?" he asked in all seriousness.

Having spent several days with this guy, I was not completely appalled at this request. "I'm afraid not. This isn't professional wrestling," I told him. "It doesn't exactly work that way."

Barely deterred, he thought for a second. "How about I send a couple of girls up to his room around midnight." He winked conspiratorially. "I'm sure we can find money in the budget for that."

I could only laugh. "Sorry."

"Then how about we media-train him?" he persisted.

I sighed. "Okay, if the player is cool with it."

So we set up a camera in a room, and the media maven spent an hour or two trying to transform this sweet, brilliant, shy SCRABBLE genius into a gregarious, charismatic spokesman. It didn't work.

It turned out to be a moot point. Our scheduled appearance was bumped two days later in the wake of a terrible airline disaster.

Probably the most challenging and complicated television experience was with the 1990 National SCRABBLE Champion, the late Robert Felt. When he won that year's event in Washington, DC, he was a veteran tournament player who had been favored to win "the big one" for a long time. Robert Felt was also one of the more interesting characters on the tournament scene.

Felt had a distinct look: a large head to hold his large brain, a doughy physique, a mass of coarse dark hair, and heavy, thick-lensed glasses. But what distinguished him the most was his ability—and tendency—to talk SCRABBLE plays and theory for hours at a time. A typical story of his might start something like this:

"I remember back in 1984 at a local tournament in Atlantic City. I was playing Tommy Tile, who I had a 17–9 lifetime record against.

Midway during the game, with the score 203–186 my favor, I draw a
rack of MBTOASW. *I see the word* WOMBATS *and a spot in the lower left*
quadrant . . ."

The guy seemed to remember every game, every opponent,
every rack, every move of his entire SCRABBLE tournament
career. And he would habitually walk up to anyone and just start
talking—and not stop. Most people listened patiently for a few
minutes, then excused themselves. Some lasted not as long and
waited to hand Felt off to an unprepared passerby. Others spotted him coming and took off.

The most famous Robert Felt anecdote took place in England, where he had gone to test his skills against the Brits. As the
story goes, a few of them were in a car as Felt was regaling the
passengers with one of these endless narratives. He was in the
midst of describing a past play when the car was sideswiped and
forced off the road, and it either spun out or actually rolled over.

But this did not deter Felt. According to the other passengers,
he never stopped telling the story, even as his fellow passengers
were screaming in fear, as the car screeched to an emergency
stop, and as the relieved passengers crawled out of the wreck. As
they dusted themselves off, they heard Felt, uninterrupted: "So
then, he draws the final S to join the blank I've tracked to be on
his rack. So I know I've got two viable options. One is a piece of
esoterica that won't play. The other is . . ."

My Robert Felt story is a little different. Let's start with his
wardrobe and overall appearance a few days before the scheduled
Good Morning America (*GMA*) appearance. Felt had arrived for
the 1990 National SCRABBLE Championship with one outfit.
It was a tattered blue oxford, faded jeans, and a pair of grubby

white sneakers. He'd also let his thick hair grow into a formless shrub, accentuating the look with a pair of enormous mutton-chop sideburns. It was a distinct look, even among a crowd of SCRABBLE experts, a number of whom couldn't have cared less about conventional style and grooming.

Felt went on to win the National SCRABBLE Championship that year, along with a $10,000 check. This was a nice payday for a man who went in and out of computer-related jobs. After the awards ceremony, we'd have approximately three hours before we had to get on a plane to New York, with a 6:30 a.m. call for *GMA*. As the clock ticked, I knew I'd have to do an emergency makeover.

To Felt's credit, he was a good sport as I rushed him to a barber for a trim and shave, then to a men's clothing store for some pants, a dress shirt, and a sports jacket. He'd use one of my ties and a pair of my shoes for the show.

That night, we made it to the hotel in New York, exhausted, but excited for the television appearance. Then, around 11:00 p.m., disaster struck.

To once again familiarize myself with the tournament story, I casually looked over the actual winning board I'd brought along. Our staff routinely took the winning board and superglued all the tiles in place. It served as a great prop for any interview, and there was always something cool about having the winning board itself in the studio.

But not this time. That's because in reviewing all the words, I noticed that DARKIE had been played in the bottom right-hand quadrant of the board. The word, of course, was an antiquated ethnic slur. To make matters worse, I'd heard from the producers that the interview was going to be conducted by Spencer Christian, an affable, beloved *GMA* weatherman, who did occasional feature pieces on the show. Spencer Christian is an African American.

By now it was nearing midnight, and I had a full-fledged dilemma on my hands. A dilemma, as once described to me, is a situation where you have two choices, neither of them great.

Fortunately, I'd learned early on to always travel with both an *Official SCRABBLE Players Dictionary* and an extra set of tiles. This discovery came the hard way early in my career—prompted by a reporter's question about a definition that had me floundering and a photographer's request for nonexistent tiles for a prop.

I found an all-night drugstore, bought some glue, and raced back to my room. Over the next hour, I carefully reconfigured part of the board. I began by changing DARKIE to DARKER. As you might expect, that involved changing some surrounding words as well. I finally finished, already dreading the next step in the process: convincing Robert Felt to go along with this. Felt, who I should mention died very young a few years later, was a SCRABBLE perfectionist. And, like a lot of top experts, he was also a purist who to some extent resented the fact that SCRABBLE was owned by a corporation, unlike games such as chess, poker, and backgammon. Many NSA members had an understandable sense of ownership of the game. They devoted their lives to it. Hasbro executives, while appreciative of SCRABBLE's legacy and genius, have scores of other games and toys to think about.

So at 6:30 a.m., I presented my case to Felt in the back of the network's limo. I mentioned that we found ourselves in an unfortunate, unanticipated, and untenable situation, but the impending interview was not the forum to address the always volatile topic of offensive words being allowed in tournament play. I closed by reminding him he'd just earned $10,000 for playing a few days of SCRABBLE, which he'd have done for free.

Robert Felt could not have been more accommodating. He totally understood the situation and accepted the reconstructed winning board as his own. The interview was wonderful. The newly groomed Felt was fabulous. I breathed a huge sigh of relief, reminding myself again that you can't always believe everything you see on television.

The story had an afterlife. I learned in later years that the word had spread among top players to never bring any suits, ties, or dress shirts to a National SCRABBLE Championship because the sponsor and the National SCRABBLE Association would add a free new wardrobe to your winnings!

7

THE WORLD JOINS IN

O VER THE YEARS, MAJOR SCRABBLE CHAMPIONSHIPS fell into one of three categories: the World SCRABBLE Championship, the National SCRABBLE Championship, and the National School SCRABBLE Championship.

All three events share much in common. Most SCRABBLE championships are held in a huge hotel ballroom or convention center event space. For the most part, all participants pay their own way to these competitions, often thousands of miles away. Every contestant knows far more words than the average English speaker—and more than likely has been learning hundreds more in the months before a big contest. Many enter knowing they have a chance to win their division; others will be thrilled to win half of their games.

The first World SCRABBLE Championship, a smaller invitational event, took place in a private club in London in 1991. There were probably fewer than 100 people in the room. By contrast, the 2004 National SCRABBLE Championship in New Orleans had nearly 850 players, plus staff, media, and onlookers for a total of nearly 1,000 people every day.

The WSC had its beginnings in Reno, Nevada—which bills itself as "the Biggest Little City in the World." Although the event itself was never held in Reno, it was the site of a historic meeting that was the genesis of this amazing tournament.

We were there the summer of 1988 for the National SCRABBLE Championship at the Sands Hotel. It was a precarious time for the culture of SCRABBLE tournament play. Selchow & Righter had sold SCRABBLE two years earlier to Coleco, a Connecticut-based company most famous for its line of Cabbage Patch Kids dolls. It turned out that by the time of the 1988 NSC, Coleco was already experiencing serious financial problems, coupled with its failed attempt to get into the personal computer business, and the company could only contribute $5,000 to the event.

As proven many times over the years, the players were undaunted by the woes, lack of interest, or financial whims of the game's manufacturer. So in the after-hours of the tournament a small group of us met to discuss our collective dream of a World SCRABBLE Championship.

On the "management" side of the table, the group consisted of the relatively new executive director of the NSA (me) and an executive at J. W. Spear & Sons, the UK-based owner of the game's worldwide rights outside of North America. Stodgy and not really a player himself, the Spear executive seemed tolerated at best by his English constituents. It was also clear that he considered me a brash Yank, poised to shake up the competitive SCRABBLE world.

Among the players from the UK—most there to play in a

US event for the first time—were Brian Sugar, Phil Appleby, Allan Simmons, and future World SCRABBLE Champion Mark Nyman. Australia was represented by John Holgate. Among the American players were, if memory serves, Mike Baron and Joe Edley.

Our agenda was short and simple with just two items. How would we resolve the dictionary differences, and who was going to host the first WSC?

The dictionary issue was which dictionary or word authority would be used to adjudicate the event: the "American," the "British," or some hybrid of both. At that time there were an estimated twenty-five thousand more words in *Chambers*, then the British word authority, than in the *Official SCRABBLE Players Dictionary* used in North America as well as selected countries such as Thailand and Australia. Think about it; the British had had the language far longer than North Americans, so it stood to reason the word source would contain a lot more words. Then, of course, there were the variants such as COLOUR for COLOR and MOULT for MOLT (to cast off an outward covering), many of which were also acceptable in North American SCRABBLE competition. It was eventually agreed that for WSC play a word had to be acceptable in either dictionary to be playable. If a word was successfully challenged, it came off the board and the player lost a turn. In order to be truly competitive for the WSC, players had to learn all or most words from both dictionaries—for North Americans an additional twenty-five thousand—and then *unlearn* them when they returned to their home country. This was a massive and cumbersome prospect, but the players did it.

In our discussion, Spear & Sons demanded that Thailand

should be banned from participating in any international event because of grievous illegal SCRABBLE manufacturing practices in that country. It was especially unfortunate that the Thai players became pawns in a commercial dispute, as SCRABBLE is arguably at least as popular in Thailand as in any other country in the world. No one knows quite how this came about, but word had it that it began when Thai leaders mandated that SCRABBLE was an official "sport" in the country and hundreds of school children were required to play in a national competition. Thai players, later admitted to compete, would go on to win the World SCRABBLE Championship—in English, their second language—in 2003 and 2009.

The process of choosing the venue for the first WSC was every bit as murky. Spear's executives were conservative by nature, and change was not something they innately embraced or pursued. Spear was a relatively lean, small family business and even though it held international trademark, remained unconvinced as to the game's true international potential.

So between Spear's cautious approach and Coleco's tenuous ownership situation, our initial meeting was inconclusive. That said, dialogue had begun, and a movement was under way.

1991 WSC, LONDON, ENGLAND

The first World SCRABBLE Championship, in London, was a landmark event for all organizers and participants. Many of us there were pinching ourselves in disbelief that the day had finally arrived.

Personally, I have an assortment of random memories. For

openers, the competition had pretty much been organized and formatted without any real input or consultation with the players themselves. As a result, there was an early elimination format that was so poorly designed that it eliminated perhaps the UK's best international player, Mark Nyman, before serious play even began.

This was a mind-boggling development to the American and Canadian players, whose sense of fair play overrode their relief at having a chief competitor eliminated. Unlike the organizers, they knew that a compromised early elimination round de-emphasized the skill factor in SCRABBLE and heightened the luck factor. Should a player get bad tiles—for example, no blanks or no s's—in a couple of consecutive games, he or she was essentially screwed. This poor planning is one of the reasons why major tournaments are well over twenty rounds, as calculations show that's when the luck factor has been mostly eliminated or brought under control.

So there we were in London when several members of the North American team decided they were going to protest the WSC format and not play at all. The most vocal was Robert Felt, who angrily maintained the tournament was now a travesty. It was 1776 all over again. The Colonies did not like the way Mother England was running things, and they were going to change it.

As I would do a few times over the years, I called an emergency meeting of the North American team, which totaled eleven players—eight Americans and three Canadians. There were also executives in attendance from the Milton Bradley Division of Hasbro, which was sponsoring and underwriting the entire trip for all of us. It goes without saying the executives were not particularly thrilled with this development. Their basic message to me was "Take care of this. And don't embarrass us."

I found an empty meeting room in the hotel and assembled the players. I began by assuring them that I completely agreed with them about the tournament's ill-conceived format. However, I reminded them of a few things.

First, we were guests in another country. It was myopic and unrealistic to assume every other culture was going to do things the same way we do. Second, our trip was underwritten by Hasbro. We owed it to them to complete the "mission." Third, carrying through with a protest would severely damage the fledgling international SCRABBLE scene before it even got started. I said the best thing we could do was play and win the first World SCRABBLE Championship.

Still several players grumbled around me. I felt like Walter Matthau in *The Bad News Bears*, managing the colorful collection of talented but nonconformist individuals. I closed the discussion by reminding them that the next such event would most certainly be hosted by us in North America, and we could format it however we chose.

And that's exactly what we did. The brilliant, modest, and sweet Peter Morris, from Lansing, Michigan, emerged victorious, becoming the first person to win both a National SCRABBLE Championship—in 1989—and a World title.

The Brits were characteristically polite, but not exactly happy with us. For openers, many thought our players were typical, pushy, talkative Americans—both in general behavior and in complaining about the format. They were also not thrilled about losing on their home turf. Hey, after all, it was *their* language. They would have their opportunity for revenge soon enough.

1993 WSC, NEW YORK, NEW YORK

We hosted the next World SCRABBLE Championship two years later, in 1993, at the world-famous Plaza Hotel in New York. The city was chosen because it was the media capital of the United States—if not the world—and all of us involved wanted to raise the profile of the event to the next level.

The opening reception began with a surprise visit from the gregarious Regis Philbin, who showed up along with his producer Michael Gelman. They'd been down the hall at an ABC function and were intrigued by the SCRABBLE signage around the hotel.

"Who knew there was such a thing as the World SCRABBLE Championship?" Regis quipped.

"Not as many people as we'd like," I told him. "That's kind of why we're here." I went on to essentially pitch Regis and Gelman the idea of someday having a SCRABBLE segment on their morning show. They said they'd think about it, as Gelman and I exchanged business cards. It took a while, but several years later we had a great piece on the *Live with Regis and Kathie Lee* show, with School SCRABBLE expert Daniel Goldman playing a match against both hosts. Daniel won handily.

Later, at the reception, I was astonished when two players from Kenya presented me with a beautiful carved ebony elephant with miniature real ivory tusks. It was about eight inches high, heavy and highly polished. It goes without saying that I was flattered. Fortunately, I found a way to repay their thoughtfulness. As we spoke, I learned that they would be staying with an African friend who was a graduate student at Rutgers in New Brunswick, New Jersey, and commuting back and forth to the event each day. They did not realize that this would probably be well over an hour's trip each way in commuter traffic! But they had no choice as they were on a bare-bones budget. In fact, one of them told me that he had sold his car in order to attend the event.

As I looked around the opulent hotel reception, it all seemed terribly unfair. The Americans, Canadians, English, and others were completely subsidized by either sponsors or their own national SCRABBLE organizations. The Kenyans had little more than the clothes on their backs and perhaps a battered dictionary stuffed into a small, worn suitcase.

However, the SCRABBLE gods were smiling on all of us. Dave Wilson, president of Hasbro Games, was in attendance hosting the event. An avuncular guy, gregarious yet tough, Dave was a veteran of decades in the game business, extremely respected throughout both the company and the industry at large.

He and I had formed a great bond over the years. Early in our relationship, he called me into his large, homey, masculine office in East Longmeadow, Massachusetts, and sat me down.

"I have just two words for you, John," he began. "*Think SCRABBLE.*"

"*Think SCRABBLE,*" I repeated mechanically.

"That's what I need you to do. Every day. See, we have scores of games here, and everyone has to juggle multiple brands and responsibilities." I knew this to be true. These guys worked their asses off.

Dave went on to explain that he wanted to know that there was always one person out there always thinking about SCRABBLE— whether it was improving the game, marketing, publicity, events, partnerships, whatever. No one at Hasbro Games had that luxury of time and focus. So tag, I was it! Until his retirement in 2005, whenever I saw Dave he'd come up to me, wink or slap me on the back and say, "Are you *thinking SCRABBLE*, John?"

My reply was always the same. "Every day, Dave. Every day."

Dave and I also agreed on a very fundamental marketing strategy for the game. It was simple: when telling the SCRABBLE story and building the brand, we should think more like chess and less like Monopoly. It was clear to us that the core properties of SCRABBLE and the perception of the game would play better from that perspective.

Back at the Plaza, I brought the two Kenyans over and introduced them to Gail Rubenstein, then Hasbro director of corporate travel, and Dave. After the players wandered off, I explained their situation. It did not take long before Dave turned to Gail.

"Do you think we can find them a room here?" he asked.

Gail smiled. "I think we can make that happen."

"And let's make sure they have room service," he added.

"Not a problem," Gail said.

We were all silent for a second, looking around the room. I spotted SCRABBLE players in turbans, saris, dashikis, yarmulkes, and more. It was Dave Wilson who spoke what we'd been thinking. He waved his arm across the room. "This is what games are really about. Not just business, not just profit and units sold. It's about people—connecting with each other through games."

So the two SCRABBLE players from Kenya spent the week at the Plaza Hotel in New York, enjoying the luxury and their room service dinners. They did not perform particularly well, but the experience was not about that.

This event at the Plaza had a few other highlights. It was, for example, the first time I personally saw a seven-letter play made right on top of another one. It was played by an Israeli competitor— distinguished by his SCRABBLE yarmulke. His play, the talk of the early rounds, was something like the plays below:

A D A P T O R

R E L E A S E

T W O S O M E

O E D I P A L

If one ever needed an example of why learning the two-letter words is so valuable, these plays pretty much provide it. Each play has one new seven-letter word and seven acceptable two-letter words.

An entirely different memory at the WSC 1993 is a practical joke at my expense. We'd been lucky enough to have been given a ridiculously large suite at the Plaza overlooking Fifth Avenue. To take advantage of this treat, my wife and business partner, Jane, and I decided to host a small cocktail party one evening during the tournament. There were perhaps twenty-five people there, including players, Hasbro execs, and international SCRABBLE association officials. Also in attendance were our longtime friends Troy and Joan Gustavson.

Troy and Joan owned and published our hometown newspaper, the *Suffolk Times*, and he was at the WSC to write a long piece about our involvement. His daughter, Sarah, and our eldest daughter, Kristen, both college students, were working as interns for the championship. The party was in full swing when I was approached by a rather reserved SCRABBLE official from Asia.

The guest bathroom was in use, he said, and he quietly, almost urgently asked me if there was another bathroom he could use. I assured him that he was welcome to use our personal bathroom in the master suite and pointed to the correct door.

He disappeared for a few minutes, then emerged from our bedroom with a strange look on his face. I waved, but he avoided my gaze. When I went over to investigate, he sort of shuffled away, proceeded to the door, and left. Perplexed, I went to the bedroom to see if there was anything wrong. As soon as I walked in, I could see the situation. It seems that my dear friend Troy had raided my closet. He'd taken four neckties from a hanger and tied one each on the four bedposts, so they basically looked like some kind of restraints used in a recent sexual escapade.

While this would have been hilarious had it been played on someone else, I was mortified. I rushed to the bed, undid the four ties from their respective posts, and stuffed them in a drawer. I had two thoughts. First, I was glad the gentleman had been the only person who'd seen this—especially considering there were newspaper reporters and Hasbro executives at the party. Second, I was wondering how I'd explain this prank to someone whose English was marginal at best. I never had the chance.

But the real story of the 1993 WSC was Mark Nyman, the newly crowned champion. Mark had established himself as a top player at a young age. He had come to New York several years earlier at age nineteen and amazingly finished second in our 1989 National SCRABBLE Championship. At just nineteen! And remember, Mark was playing with the "American" dictionary, which put him at a distinct disadvantage. It was truly one of the most astonishing tournament SCRABBLE performances in history.

Mark was everything you'd want in a SCRABBLE champion. He was young, handsome, polite, humble, and brilliant and liked to enjoy himself. We had become fast friends and socialized whenever our paths crossed in Europe or North America. He played a remarkable tournament and came from two games behind to defeat a former North American champion, Canadian Joel Wapnick, in a best-of-five finals.

The finals were being televised closed-circuit to a ballroom audience of perhaps two hundred people, including all eliminated players, officials, invited guests, media, Hasbro execs, and hotel staff who'd become fascinated during the event. The intensity was palpable as we watched the two players in perhaps the highest-stakes match of their lives. At one point, with the outcome still in question, Nyman leaned back in his chair, then forward again. Without breaking his serious expression, Mark picked up a pencil and scribbled something on his notepad.

The entire audience leaned forward in their chairs, straining to see what he'd written. As the camera went in for a close-up, we finally saw Nyman's note. It read: "I'D FANCY A PINT." The entire room went crazy with laughter.

Minutes later, Mark Nyman went on to win the game and the tournament. He and Wapnick entered the ballroom to a standing ovation and climbed up to the podium for the award ceremony. A weary and happy Mark strode up to the microphone as the applause slowly died down. At last, he looked around the room, leaned into the mike, and said, "I seem to be at a loss for words." The crowd again erupted in laughter.

As one might expect, the Brits were ready to celebrate after capturing their first World SCRABBLE Championship. Not only had they avenged their previous defeat in London, they'd done so in dramatic, elegant fashion. That evening, a group of us—

Americans, Canadians, and Brits—had a glorious Indian dinner together. Afterward, most of us were exhausted and headed to our rooms. But not Mark. He and a couple of his best mates were going to keep the party going. As they headed out into the night, I reminded Mark that we had a 6:45 a.m. pickup for *Good Morning America*. "Not to worry, John," he shouted happily as he crawled into the back of a waiting taxicab.

And I didn't worry—until about 6:00 a.m. Mark Nyman was missing. I called his room at the hotel—no answer. I called the head of the UK SCRABBLE team—no idea. Then the calls started coming to me. First it was the limo driver waiting outside the Plaza for us. Then it was a producer from *Good Morning America*. Then it was the limo driver again.

By 7:00 a.m. I was starting to get frantic. Obviously, I was worried about my young English friend, out for a night on the town in New York, a city he and his companions did not know particularly well. I resisted thinking about all the grim fates that might have befallen Mark in an unforgiving Manhattan night.

Of course, the professional side of me was worried as well. As always, it was understood that I would deliver the latest SCRABBLE champion to one of the "morning shows." As mentioned earlier, this exposure was worth millions of dollars in publicity for SCRABBLE, more than justifying the expense of the entire tournament. As we approached 7:15 a.m., I knew I was in jeopardy of losing our segment.

And then there were my all-important sartorial concerns—for Mark Nyman had borrowed my favorite suit and tie for the television appearance! Fortunately, there was a happy ending. Mark showed up around 7:30 a.m., cheerful, apologetic, and a tad weary. Yet he absolutely aced the interview before heading back to the Plaza for a much-needed and well-deserved nap.

1995 WSC, LONDON, ENGLAND

In 1995, the World SCRABBLE Championship returned to London. It was held at the beautiful Park Lane Hotel near Hyde Park, and the Brits went all out in regard to amenities and hospitality. There was even the first—and last—semiformal dinner dance in the history of tournament SCRABBLE! The word SURREAL came to mind as I rocked out on the dance floor with my thirteen-year-old daughter, Alex, an array of SCRABBLE experts from two dozen countries flailing around us.

One of the more curious aspects of this event was the presence of rock star Robert Palmer, who had signed on as official greeter/ambassador. Palmer, a handsome, smooth, and affable guy, was best known to most of us as the star of the "Simply Irresistible" video. First aired in 1988, it was one of the most seminal rock videos in history. It featured Palmer, in a handsome suit and silver tie, backed up by half a dozen or so identical, gorgeous dark-haired models who stared blankly into the camera while allegedly playing various musical instruments.

My wife and I spent a fair amount of time with Palmer and his girlfriend at lunch and during the off-hours. It became clear that the rocker had a tangential relationship with SCRABBLE at best and was there to have some fun and pick up some extra cash because some PR or marketing exec decided the event needed a celebrity to offset the staid image of SCRABBLE. It was refreshing to see Palmer be a good sport about it all and a real gentleman.

The 1995 London World SCRABBLE Championship was ultimately won by Canadian David Boys. He defeated American Joel Sherman in the finals to collect the trophy and the seemingly random $11,000 first prize. The field had now grown from the initial nineteen countries to thirty-one. I liked the fact that the WSC had been won by American Peter Morris, Englishman Mark Nyman, and now Canadian David Boys. Only later did someone point out that Peter Morris was born in Manchester, England, and had Canadian citizenship as well.

1997 WSC, WASHINGTON, DC

We selected Washington, DC, for the 1997 World SCRABBLE Championships for all the obvious reasons. It is another great media town. It's easy to get to. And we could rely on the diplomatic corps to add an even more prominent international theme to the competition.

The Mayflower Hotel in the heart of the city was our chosen site. Like the Plaza Hotel before it, the Mayflower was gorgeous, historical, and prestigious. On our first visit to inspect the hotel, the Secret Service was all over the place in preparation for an event a few nights later that President Bill Clinton would be attending. I knew it was just a matter of time before someone asked me if we could arrange for the president to drop by the tournament. It had been reported numerous times in the press that the Clintons were big SCRABBLE fans.

It was warm in Washington when the NSA staff arrived the day before the competition began. From the moment we landed we were consumed with the ballroom setting up, fielding press calls, assembling contestant materials and gifts, tracking down packages, tracing missing players, and more. Later, I went to bed early after dinner but was wide awake at 1:30 a.m. and had trouble going back to sleep. Restless, I decided to get dressed and go down to the lobby and out for a walk.

The lobby was understandably empty, with the exception of one man who was in the process of checking in. He caught my attention both by his mere presence at that hour and by his appearance. He was tall and lean with deep tan skin and pale blue eyes, framed by a shock of silver hair. He wore a rumpled suit and had a large distressed-leather suitcase at his feet. It was held together by a piece of rope.

Eavesdropping, I learned he had just arrived from the Middle East to compete in the World SCRABBLE Championship. I decided not to introduce myself quite yet and proceeded outside for a walk around the block. My head was spinning with gratitude for being so deeply and personally involved with SCRABBLE. That a simple game could have that kind of appeal for people all over the world was profound.

The competition, as always, was intense and dazzling. The final, for the first time in the history of the event, would be an all-American affair. It featured "G.I. Joel" Sherman against fellow New Yorker Matt Graham.

This was a matchup with built-in drama and personalities worthy of professional wrestling or a comic-book superhero showdown. Sherman is a sweet, self-effacing homebody. Graham, a stand-up comic, is brash, athletic, and intense. I liked both of them very much and considered them friends. Joel was a longtime expert, one of the few who'd ultimately win both a National and World SCRABBLE Championship. Matt was a well-known SCRABBLE gambler, looking for validation among the SCRABBLE elite by winning his first major title.

It was an exciting final, with Joel prevailing. But for me, the interesting part came after it was all over. I learned that Matt—always the gambler—had approached Joel before the final and suggested a deal. The proposal was that they combine the first-prize money of $25,000 and the second-prize money of $10,000 and split the total right down the middle. I'm not sure what Matt's motivation was—a sure thing? In some ways, it made sense for both of them. Matt had left his job writing for *Saturday Night Live* and lived simply in perhaps New York's smallest apartment. He supported himself on a meager income from comedy gigs, writing, and help from friends.

Joel's financial situation was humble as well. He lived with his brother and father in the same house in the Bronx where he grew up. Various conditions kept him from being regularly employed, and he subsisted on a small inheritance and SCRABBLE winnings. Joel recalled later that he'd anticipated Matt's scheme—but he rejected it. Matt could not have been completely surprised.

1999 WSC, MELBOURNE, AUSTRALIA

For the 1999 World SCRABBLE Championship, we took things Down Under—to Melbourne, Australia. This was significant in several ways. For openers, it signaled that the sponsors, Hasbro and Mattel, were committed to making the event even more global. (Mattel had purchased Spear & Sons and the new international rights to SCRABBLE outside of North America.) Sure,

London, New York, and Washington were great and necessary to get things started. But choosing Melbourne brought the international aspect to an entirely new level. It allowed all of us in the SCRABBLE community to dream of future competitions in India, Canada, Bermuda, Hong Kong—all former British colonies and emblematic of the vast reach of the English language.

Clearly, the international scene was growing, albeit incrementally. As we saw it, our success was also reflective of the world's increasing desire to assimilate English. I'd like to think that was true. But let's face it; there are easier and more practical ways to learn English than by becoming an international SCRABBLE tournament player. Hell, half the words you learn would never even appear in everyday conversation. After all, when was the last time you heard a pal casually mention QAID (a Muslim leader, also spelled CAID), CWM (a deep-walled basin), or HAPKIDO (a Korean martial art)?

I'd never been to Australia and was thrilled for the opportunity, as was my wife. She was photographing the event and sending constant updates to NSA webmaster John Chew in Toronto, who posted them. Thanks to John's programming, we got over six million hits on the NSA website during the event.

After a couple of days exploring Sydney, we made our way to Melbourne for the championship. Mattel's Philip Nelkon, my international counterpart, had arranged a beautiful suite for us in the gorgeous Carlton Crest Hotel.

Here we were, thousands of miles from New York, and the first thing we saw—and heard—when we arrived at the hotel was "G.I. Joel" Sherman playing the piano in the lobby. Nearby, several SCRABBLE games were under way; players from all over the world had reconnected, exchanged pleasantries, and then jumped right into playing. There was a good chance some of them had not even unpacked yet.

As in previous years, the opening reception was a wondrous whirl of diverse accents, national dress, and SCRABBLE ability. Again, I was astonished that fully three-quarters of the field of '98 didn't have a chance in hell of winning the tournament and most would be thrilled to win just half their games. I thought, too, how the World SCRABBLE Championship was a mirror of the world at large. Once again the Western nationals were well financed, while the Africans had made extraordinary sacrifices just to be there.

For example, one of Nigeria's most prominent players would finish every tournament and pretty much beg fellow players and organizers for spare boards, tiles, and other equipment. Nigerians were rabid about SCRABBLE, but games were hard to come by, even for those who could afford them. Blessed with good fortune, both our players and the NSA gladly gave him all we could.

One of the African champions once asked me if the National SCRABBLE Association could help him seek and obtain political asylum. While I'd become accustomed to pretty much anything crossing my desk over the years, this was a new one for me. A brief conversation with the State Department put a quick end to that endeavor.

At the 1999 WSC, I received two more unusual gifts, from the two players from Romania. One is a small triangular silk pennant emblazoned with three multicolored SCRABBLE tiles—F, S, and R. Above the graphic is the proud copy FEDERATIA DE ROMANA DE SCRABBLE. It has hung in my office for nearly fifteen years. It was explained to me that the Romanian English SCRABBLE Association had approximately fourteen members.

The other was a very good bottle of wine from, of all places, the Transylvanian region. Its label was rich scarlet, deep green, and bold gray and featured a leering portrait of Count Dracula. It was, of course, a dark, full-bodied red wine.

The 1999 World SCRABBLE Championship was won by longtime SCRABBLE expert Joel Wapnick, a music professor at McGill University in Montreal. With this well-earned victory, Joel joined the list of players to win both the National SCRABBLE Championship (1983) and the World SCRABBLE Championship. It was a long time coming for Joel, legendary for his word knowledge, and a group of us celebrated that evening miles away from home with a beachside sunset dinner at one of Melbourne's better restaurants.

2001 WSC, LAS VEGAS, NEVADA

The 2001 World SCRABBLE Championship, held at the lavish Venetian Hotel in Las Vegas, would be my most memorable for a number of reasons. For openers, unbeknownst to me, it would be the last WSC we at the National SCRABBLE Association would ever organize, attend, and publicize. And in many ways, it will remain the most dramatic WSC in history, chiefly because of the timing. Over a year in advance, it had been scheduled for November 13, 2001—which ended up being just two months and two days after the 9/11 attacks that pretty much changed the world as we knew it.

As one might expect, initially it was widely assumed that the tournament would be canceled after the attacks. The world was still cloaked in mourning, uncertainty, and fear. No one wanted to fly. No one—from everyday people to large corporations—wanted to spend money frivolously. And the idea of simply having fun or celebrating *anything* seemed impossible and almost heretical. For Americans of a certain age, it was evocative of Pearl Harbor or the Kennedy assassination, a watershed "End of the Innocence" event that sent us reeling into a collective emotional dark hole.

Despite all the reservations about holding the World SCRABBLE Championship, it was decided we would proceed as planned. The opportunity to host a positive international event at this time was just too powerful to ignore. Sure, it was only a SCRABBLE tournament—we got that—but it was a start.

Before 9/11, we had representatives from over thirty-five countries registered to play. When we contacted them all after 9/11, every single one renewed the commitment to attend! Also of sudden significance was the fact that we'd have players from Iraq, Israel, Pakistan, Qatar, and Saudi Arabia.

However, we had made one critical error in our planning. As with any big event, we had checked the calendar for conflicts with Thanksgiving, Christmas, the Jewish holidays, the Olympics, elections, and everything else we could think of—except for Ramadan, the most holy of Muslim holidays. The way our schedule stood, we'd be forcing the Muslim players to compete on a day when they should be fasting and praying.

This oversight was brought to my attention in a registered letter from the president of the Pakistan SCRABBLE Association. Obviously, the timing could not have been worse. I had no excuse other than that I was—like most other Americans—embarrassingly ignorant about both the Arab world and Muslims. About all

I knew was that not all Muslims were Arabs and vice versa. The Pakistani SCRABBLE executive was very gracious in excusing my oversight. I assured him it would never happen again.

It goes without saying that security was a huge consideration. We'd had some experience with security issues over the years. As I mentioned, I received a death threat from a zealous word lover who was disappointed that words were removed from the SCRABBLE dictionary. A woman player had secured an order of protection against a SCRABBLE-playing male stalker. Then there were the random temper tantrums when players had to be escorted off the playing floor to calm down.

But the 2001 WSC security concerns were a little different. For one thing, we were in Las Vegas. While the city is a fun place for most of us, religious fanatics of all persuasions consider Vegas pretty much Satan's hometown. What better place to make some big politico-religious statement? Also, the fact that people from nearly three dozen countries were being "forced" to play the game in English—viewed by some as the language of Oppressors—might rub certain fringe thinkers the wrong way. Looking back, I realize the craziness of the time made us look at things in a way we'd never imagined. We still do.

Our fears were put to rest at pre-event meetings, when we were reminded that a top Las Vegas hotel probably has security as good as the White House. So by the time we arrived at the Venetian we were very comfortable, and it was our job to make our guests feel the same.

Another surprise awaited us as we checked in to the hotel. It was cowboys—hundreds and hundreds of cowboys. While scheduling the 2001 WSC, we'd somehow failed to discover that Las Vegas has a gigantic annual rodeo. The extravaganza is attended by tens of thousands of people—almost every one of them staying at the Venetian Hotel, apparently.

The entire championship, one couldn't walk anywhere around the hotel without being surrounded by scores of guys wearing cowboy hats. This was especially amusing to the foreign SCRABBLE competitors. For many of them, this was their first trip to America—so seeing everyone walking around in cowboy hats confirmed their preconceived image of Americans. All that was missing was guns.

We opened the tournament with a welcoming reception with a total of eighty-eight players from thirty-five countries participating. Some of the players, most playing in their second or even third language, impressively came from these exotic destinations: Bahrain, Cameroon, Gibraltar, Guyana, India, Israel, Kenya, Kurdistan-Iraq, Malaysia, Malta, Oman, Philippines, Qatar, Saudi Arabia, Singapore, South Africa, Sri Lanka, Tanzania, Trinidad and Tobago, and Zambia.

The mood was a mix of cautious excitement, anticipation, and reflection. As players and guests arrived, the NSA staff formed a reception line at the entrance to the room. There were series of heartfelt hugs from strangers and a lot of teary-eyed conversations and reunions. It goes without saying that 9/11 was on everyone's mind, and I knew I had to address the topic in my opening remarks.

I'd learned early in my SCRABBLE career that I should always keep my remarks brief, but they were even shorter than anticipated. That's because the sound system wasn't working, despite every effort to fix it. Yet I needed to be heard by three hundred people, many of whom were still talking among themselves. Finally, I pulled a chair up to the center of the room and stood on it. My wife, Jane, who has one of the strongest, most shrill New York "taxi" whistles around, silenced the room with one piercing screech.

The large room fell silent. On behalf of the NSA and Hasbro, I thanked all the players for their sacrifice and commitment, especially given the turbulence of the times. I reminded them that although our group was small in number, we represented the diversity and good in the world and what can happen when peoples work together. That was it. I jumped off the chair and faded into the crowd. The first person to approach me was my seventy-eight-year-old father, who was attending his first—and, sadly, last— SCRABBLE tournament. A former Nazi prisoner of war for three and a half years in World War II—at the notorious Stalag 17 POW camp—he was no stranger to international tension. "Nice job," he said. My father was a guy who dispensed compliments at about five per lifetime, so it meant a lot to me.

The 2001 WSC was arguably one of the most amazing in the history of the event. Fittingly, since it was to be the last ever held on North American soil, the Americans and Canadians more than made their presence felt. They ended up taking seven of the top ten places, including the final, which pitted defending champ Joel Wapnick, a Canadian, against Chicago's Brian Cappelletto.

A little background on Brian. As I write this, he has permanently retired from tournament play, which is a huge loss for the game. Brian is a brilliant player, a really good sport, and a genuinely nice guy. He was the first of just a handful of tournament SCRABBLE "prodigies."

Cap—as he's called—first got everyone's attention at sixteen years old, when he began to beat established SCRABBLE masters on a regular basis. One of the very first experts to realize Brian's potential was the legendary SCRABBLE player, promoter, and author Mike Baron, from New Mexico. Mike is well-known for authoring *The SCRABBLE Wordbook*, the first comprehensive must-have volume for all tournament SCRABBLE players. It essentially presents all two- to eight-letter words in various lists and categories that make them easier to study and memorize.

Asked to recall the early days when Brian Cappelletto first came on the scene, Mike had this to say: "I had the pleasure of meeting Brian in his first tournament, in October 1985. He had just turned sixteen, and it was my thirty-sixth birthday. I thought I'd have an easy win. But Brian played aggressively, in a brash style the likes of which I'd never seen before, playing into the triple-word columns, exposing multiple hook spots, playing words no newcomer to the game had a right to know. Only by a lure and a challenged word (HEPS) was I able to eke out a 414–407 victory in our first match."

Always putting the good of the game ahead of his personal goals, Baron promptly sent the young Cappelletto some of his valuable word lists for study. "It was," noted Baron wryly, "ammunition he would soon use against me time and again."

Like many prodigies in various endeavors, Brian became a victim of his own potential. Many players assumed that he'd win a national championship sooner rather than later—possibly in his teens. Well, that didn't happen. It wasn't because Brian didn't have the talent, skill, and will to win. It was, many observers felt, because he hadn't reached the requisite level of maturity yet.

After thirty years of observing the best SCRABBLE players in the world, I've come to believe that the spiritual/emotional component is an absolute key to being a champion. There are many players who have all or most of the SCRABBLE dictionary memorized. An equal number can anagram a ten-letter word in a nanosecond. Then there are others whose strategic thinking is almost flawless. Yet none of them will ever become a World or National Champion, because they can't quite achieve the level of calmness and maturity a champion needs.

Most SCRABBLE champions do not get overly excited when they win a game, nor do they punch holes in a wall when they lose. They do not fret about their current standing in a tournament or masochistically replay bad moves from an earlier game. They do not look ahead to upcoming games. Instead, they keep their focus in the game they are playing. Sure, anyone can draw bad tiles, but having the wrong mental approach—or none at all—is one of the few ways a player can beat him or herself. Besides carrying a bad loss into the next game, this might include being too cavalier about the time clock, trying too hard to psych out your opponent, or worrying about how your rivals are doing in the standings.

Brian Cappelletto finally got the proverbial monkey off his back when he won the 1998 National Championship in Chicago at age twenty-nine. Even better, he *lived* in Chicago, which was both convenient and media-worthy.

In Las Vegas, Brian had the opportunity to laminate his legacy with a win at the 2001 World SCRABBLE Championship. There was just one obstacle in his way, and he went by the name of Joel Wapnick. It goes without saying all of us were beyond excited that the finals would pit two of the greatest players in history against each other.

They did not disappoint. The first game was a nail-biter, with Wapnick winning at the very end by 3 points, 482–479. Consider it: a game of almost 1,000 total points decided by 3 points!

Word lovers were not disappointed either, as each player dredged up some spectacular plays from his arsenal of esoterica. Wapnick played WHEEP (to give forth a prolonged whistle) and BAJU (a short jacket worn in Malaysia)—a word not even acceptable in North America! (Wapnick knew it from international play.) Brian, for his part, played INDUSIA (an enveloping layer or membrane). I can state with certainty that I had never seen that word before and have not seen it since.

Though Joel won that first game, Brian went on to win the next three in a row to capture the title and take home the $25,000 first prize. He joined Peter Morris, Joel Sherman, and Wapnick as the only players at that point in history to have won both Worlds and Nationals. (Nigel Richards would achieve this later.) Like Peter Morris, Brian would retire early from the game, in his case to pursue a business career. Yet his place in SCRABBLE lore is intact. In fact, over the years I asked many experts this question: If you had to name one player who is just a bit better than everyone else, who would it be? Their answer would almost always be "Brian." What exactly earned Brian this distinction? Basically, he brought the whole skill set when he sat down at the board. For openers, he'd been playing at the expert level since he was a teenager—so he'd seen it all and was not intimidated by any opponent or situation. He knew almost the entire dictionary. His board vision and strategic skills were as good as anyone's. And he was calm and calculating in every game.

Brian Cappelletto's place in SCRABBLE tournament history would be eclipsed with the emergence of Nigel Richards. A quiet New Zealander who works in Malaysia as a security consultant, Nigel has dominated the World and National SCRABBLE

Championships in recent years. He's won the NSC five times as of this writing and the WSC three times. And Nigel is far from finished.

I remember Joe Edley telling me many years ago, "There's this new player named Nigel Richards who will definitely win a World Championships someday and may have more potential than anyone I've ever seen."

Nigel brings an impressive arsenal to every game and no apparent weaknesses. He's alleged to have a true photographic memory, knowing every word in both the "American" and international dictionaries. Don't try a phony word on this guy! He may also be the most placid competitor I've ever seen. It's impossible to tell by looking at him whether he is ahead or behind, or, for that matter, whether he's just won or lost a game. Nigel has said more than once that he really doesn't care that much about winning or losing; he simply loves to play.

Nigel also epitomizes the mind/body connection espoused by champions in many pursuits. I remember a National SCRABBLE Championship in Dallas where he had booked a hotel room over twenty miles away from the event. Each day for almost a week, he rode his bike to the tournament, played SCRABBLE for six or eight hours, went out to dinner, and then pedaled back to his hotel. Oh yeah, it was during a heat wave when the Dallas temperatures hit triple digits a number of times. And yes, Nigel won that championship as well.

■ ■ ■

After the 2001 WSC both Hasbro and Mattel decided to either scale back or eliminate their financial support for an international event. In mid-2013, it was announced that a third-party company called Mind Sports International would take over organizing and promoting the World SCRABBLE Championship. As described in the UK SCRABBLE newsletter, the company is "the driving force behind the internationally recognized Mind Sports Festival, which takes place in fantastic locations around the world, whilst working to promote all of the positive aspects behind intellectual sports in a bid to help increase popularity of these games with both new and established players."

It was also announced that the World SCRABBLE Championship would be renamed the SCRABBLE Champions Tournament, presumably for legal reasons. The first event, with a guaranteed first prize of $10,000, took place in Prague in late 2013. That the WSC would go through this metamorphosis and end up in the adopted home of Franz Kafka is priceless. As they say, you can't make this stuff up. The 2013 SCRABBLE Champions was won by Nigel Richards. Brit Craig Beevers won in 2014.

8

MAN VS. MACHINE

O NE OF THE BEST THINGS TO come out of World SCRABBLE Championships was a challenge match in May 1998 that teamed the top two finishers of the 1997 WSC, Joel Sherman and Matt Graham, together in a best-of-nine showdown against something called "Maven," at that time the state-of-the-art SCRABBLE software program. It was inspired by two highly publicized chess matches between IBM's program "Deep Blue" and international chess master Garry Kasparov, who won the first match, in 1996, and lost the rematch a year later.

The SCRABBLE Man vs. Machine match was first proposed to me by my friend John Tierney, an author and veteran *New York Times* columnist. An excellent SCRABBLE player himself, John wanted to stage the match for a long piece in a *New York Times* Sunday magazine. It would be titled "Humankind Battles for Scrabble Supremacy." (A wonderful in-depth article, it appeared on May 24, 1998, and is available online.)

The event would be sponsored by the *Times* as part of

SCRABBLE's ongoing Fiftieth Anniversary celebration. Obviously, all of us involved jumped at the chance.

As preparations began for the match, we had numerous considerations. Chief among these were our expectations. In theory, the human race would have a better chance with SCRABBLE than with chess because of the luck factor. Chess is all skill; the better man or machine should win. SCRABBLE is, by most accounts, 15 percent luck. Backgammon has been estimated at around the same as SCRABBLE. Based on my admittedly scant research, no one seems to agree on the luck factor in poker.

So if the human team of Matt and Joel drew reasonable tiles, it would be a competitive match. On the other side, the computer would have the entire dictionary completely at its disposal, mistake-free with no wrong guesses. Maven would also have a bit of a psychological advantage—if that's even possible for artificial intelligence. The advantage? Speed. It was more than likely that teammates Matt and Joel would have to carefully evaluate every move, discuss it, and then agree. It was also entirely possible they might disagree on the best move, with one guy ultimately caving in and conceivably pouting. Perhaps I'm exaggerating here, but the point is real. Never underestimate the subtle, corrosive damage a bad SCRABBLE move can do to the human ego and psyche.

So that was our reality. Maven, being soulless, did not have this potential liability. To perform well, Matt and Joel would need to find and agree on their best play. Maven could and would counter every move of its human opponents within two seconds. That could be disheartening at best.

So a group of us gathered in the penthouse of the old New York Times Building on West Forty-third Street in Manhattan.

It was a cavernous space, with high ceilings, windows overlooking the city, and scores of artifacts and artworks that chronicled the paper's history. There was a bar and kitchen area, beautiful rugs, and antique furniture as well. Looking around, I tried to imagine all the various functions that had been held here, populated with authors, presidents, tycoons, celebrities, and the like. And now it was SCRABBLE players. Us.

Our group included, of course, Joel Sherman, Matt Graham, and John Tierney. Also invited was NSA staff member and three-time National SCRABBLE Champion Joe Edley, who would serve as the official and word judge. This was curious, as Edley would be watching closely, doubtlessly second-guessing some of the plays of his colleagues. Hey, bring on the drama!

We'd also invited Brian Sheppard, the genius MIT computer programmer who invented Maven. We'd flown him down from Cambridge for the historic event. A polite, unassuming guy, Brian had not been a serious SCRABBLE player when he began to invent the world's best nonhuman SCRABBLE player. Yet through the experience of the project Brian—almost through osmosis—became a top-rated expert. He played his first tournament game in October of 1987 and his last in December of 1990. He achieved a rating of 1840 after just two events, placing him comfortably in the Top 100 ranking among all North American competitors. Also in attendance was Eric Chaikin, who a few years later would go on to codirect and produce the documentary *Word Wars*. It premiered at the Sundance Film Festival in 2004 and was later nominated for an Emmy. Eric's film featured both Joel Sherman and Matt Graham as central characters.

Rounding out the spectators was my friend Beth Balsam, an executive at Fleishman-Hilliard, Hasbro's PR agency for games and other activities. A serious SCRABBLE lover, Beth made what may have been the play of the day. We were all hanging out at lunch playing anagrams. The topic was common words that anagrammed into names of celebrities. For example, one was PRESBYTERIAN, which amusingly rearranges to BRITNEY SPEARS.

We were all staring at the word NARCOLEPTIC when Beth blurted out "ERIC CLAPTON." A collective gasp nearly sucked the air out of the room. As Beth herself told me, "It was great. No one could believe that the friggin' PR woman came up with the answer first!"

"Yeah," I replied, "that one's definitely going on your lifetime highlight reel along with your wedding day and the birth of your first child."

The match itself was fascinating. Just before we began, I told Matt and Joel, "Not to add any pressure, but the entire human race is counting on you guys." In reality, no one could put more pressure on these guys than themselves. Confidence was another matter. Matt was convinced they had both the ability and experience to beat Maven. Joel thought they were evenly matched at best.

For me, there were a couple of vivid recollections. One was perhaps among the most amazing plays I'd ever seen. It was close to midway during the best-of-eleven match. Matt and Joel were trailing and had worked hard to come up with a good play in a crucial game. Maven, true to form, took a second and then threw down the word TIRAMISU for a gazillion points. Matt and Joel exchanged shocked, wounded looks and slumped in their chairs. Personally, I felt it was the deciding play of the entire day; there was no way these guys were going to win. I mean, really, think of the construction of that word. An eight-letter bad boy ending in

U? Is there any other eight-letter word ending in U in the entire language? If so, Maven could tell us in 1.5 seconds.

Then there was the inevitable shouting match between Matt and Joel as they started to fall behind. They essentially disagreed about the choice of a particular play, each convinced his move was the best. It became so contentious that I had to stop play for several minutes so the human beings could cool off. Maven, for his part, remained predictably nonplussed. It was quite a contrast: two agitated humans arguing in front of and gesturing toward their opponent—a computer and screen on top of a table. The match lasted nine games, with Maven winning 6–3. Matt and Joel had played as well as possible considering they were matched against an opponent with total, perfect word knowledge. Indeed, the guys made some brilliant, subtle plays that Maven could never have "seen" as they had not been programmed into its strategic DNA—yet. Most importantly, everyone in the room, including Maven inventor Brian Sheppard, agreed that Maven had clearly benefited by better tiles during the course of the day. So far, there has been no rematch.

■　■　■

However, humankind did get revenge a few years later when 2006 National SCRABBLE Champion Jim Kramer defeated the "Genius" SCRABBLE program from Real Networks in a best-of-three match in Seattle in an outdoor setting. "Gentleman Jim" is the former proofreader of the *SCRABBLE News*. He took home $10,000 for the win.

9

THE SCHOOL
SCRABBLE PROGRAM

YOU HAVEN'T LIVED UNTIL YOU'VE SEEN a group of twelve-year-old boys fighting over a dictionary. Nearly twenty years ago I witnessed this, along with a group of astonished teachers and parents in Springfield, Massachusetts.

The boys—in jeans, sports jerseys, and backward baseball caps—were taking part in a SCRABBLE tournament for local middle schools from all over the region. A disputed play had emerged during their match, and four boys ran over to the nearest dictionary and began a playful tug-of-war to see who could find the word first. "If I wasn't watching this myself," a nearby teacher whispered, "I never would have believed it."

That incident pretty much epitomized the mission and spirit of the National School SCRABBLE Program. It is probably the single most meaningful accomplishment in my twenty-five-plus years at the National SCRABBLE Association. Here's how it began.

By 1990, it was clear to us at the NSA that we were going to have to devise a plan and course of action to create the next generation of SCRABBLE consumers and players. The America that spawned the initial SCRABBLE craze back in the early 1950s barely existed anymore. The days of Mom, Dad, Grandma, and the kids sitting around the kitchen table playing board games seemed doomed. The norm had switched to single-parent households, working mothers, MTV, and powerful new distractions such as the Internet and cell phones.

Since we could no longer safely assume kids would be introduced to board games in the family setting, we had to find fun, effective alternative ways to expose them to SCRABBLE. We knew the best way would be through schools.

This was easier said than done. Justifiably, American educators are extremely dubious about letting any commercial interest infiltrate the sanctity of the classroom. It was one thing—already controversial—to have vending machines in school cafeterias selling soft drinks, chips, and candy. Bringing a commercial product into a classroom and having students sample it was a far more challenging prospect. The only large-scale precedent and successful venture of the kind we knew of was when Apple donated computers to schools back in 1975.

Still, there were at least two factors that I knew could work in our favor. First, for better or worse, SCRABBLE was often perceived as a generic "brand" like chess, bingo, backgammon, and cards. The idea that it was a product owned and zealously guarded by a large corporation never even entered people's minds. To them, SCRABBLE was just another piece of the American culture—like baseball. Most everybody owned a board. Most everybody had played it at least once or twice. SCRABBLE had just always been there.

I calculated that this de-commercialized image of the game would help us counter any resistance from educators. I also knew that between word-loving teachers and parents, and thousands of NSA members throughout the country, we would have a motivated force of individuals to serve as our foot soldiers in this initiative. But the overwhelming selling point for the fledgling School SCRABBLE Program was the innate and obvious educational value of the game itself.

The learning aspects of SCRABBLE were twofold: the obvious and the subtle. The obvious included spelling and vocabulary. The less obvious were math, spatial relationships, decision-making, and "cooperative learning." The latter is a term for teamwork: students work in pairs or small groups on a specific learning task or project in an effort to organize classroom activities into social and learning experiences.

SCRABBLE is in many ways about math. In School SCRABBLE, kids have to keep a running score, which includes basic addition. They have to apply multiplication in calculating a specific move. And they quickly learn the core skill of figuring probability by knowing how many of a certain letter have been played and how many remain in the bag or on an opponent's rack.

Spatial relationships and decision-making are learned by developing board vision—seeing every possible play in every place on the board. At any given time, a player has numerous options all over the board for making a play, and the best play is not always about the most points. So we knew kids would learn critical thinking by having to both identify and evaluate their options. We introduced this concept in a very simple way. In classroom testing, we had each student find the tiles for his or her name and place it on the board, then move it around to cover various bonus squares. They quickly understood it was worth different values in different places. Bingo!

The cooperative learning aspect was extremely interesting, and underestimated in the School SCRABBLE Program. If one accepts the premise that competition and life at large are not always about winning, it makes sense. Our overriding belief was this: if the School SCRABBLE Program was not fun above all else, it would fail. That's why we decided early on to have the kids play in pairs. For one thing, it would substantially limit the intimidation factor. No one likes to look stupid, especially middle school students; teaming kids up, we gave them a built-in sense of comfort by partnership. For another, some kids were better at spelling, others at the math side of the game, so teamwork maximized the chances for success.

Teachers soon learned to pair up kids in experimental ways: a shy kid with an extrovert, the class bully with a nerd, a black kid with a white kid, and so on. We collected a huge amount of anecdotal research. A long-term goal was to hire a team of educational experts to track two different classes for an entire school year. One group would participate heavily in SCRABBLE, both after school and in the classroom. The other would conduct their studies as always. After a year, testing would be devised to see how the former group matched up with the latter in spelling, vocabulary, dictionary use, math, and other more abstract skills such as collaborative ability and even attention span. (I should emphasize that this is a simplification of what the study would have been, had it progressed beyond the talking stage.)

A wonderful example of the collaborative aspect of cooperative learning emerged from a middle school in Pennsylvania during our early testing phases before the program launch. It featured a twelve-year-old boy who had been deemed a "distraction" to other students because of erratic behavior. As a result, he was routinely marginalized from the general student population. He spent his days in an empty classroom with a tutor who also served as a monitor.

However, his School SCRABBLE Program teacher had the idea to have him participate in a session. After he was paired with a compatible partner, the experiment began. It could not have turned out any better. The boy immediately took to SCRABBLE and was thoroughly engaged. Better yet, he was a calm, focused partner. Encouraged by the initial progress, the teachers continued the experiment. His behavior continued to improve. Ultimately, they decided to take things further. The boy was introduced into an art class, where he was given a partner on a simple project. It worked! He was comfortable, engaged, productive, and increasingly social. I'm not saying he went on to be the valedictorian or president of the student body—I have no idea—but these were critical baby steps. And no path to wholeness or self-improvement starts without them.

Before the national launch of the program, our NSA-Hasbro team took our idea on the road to various schools for nearly two years to see what we could learn. Geographically, we chose three regions: the Springfield, Massachusetts area, Long Island, and Manhattan. Hasbro Games was located in East Longmeadow, a few miles away from Springfield. In many ways, it could be Anywhere, USA, which was exactly what we wanted. Long Island, where the NSA was headquartered, served as the testing ground for suburban and rural schools, and Manhattan would provide the urban experience. To be thorough, we agreed we had to visit classrooms from grades 1–12 in both public and private schools.

We had decided we needed three trips to every school. The initial trip was to introduce ourselves and the fundamentals of the game. The second was to give some advanced tips and begin competition. The third was to have an informal class championship. Bear in mind we were teaching the teacher as well.

It was clear on the first visit to grades 1–3 that they were not the ideal participants. Though sweet and cute, the kids were predictably distracted and fidgety. Despite being up for the new experience, they soon became bored. Also, their vocabularies and maturity were simply too undeveloped for them to find plays easily and quickly. I should add there were numerous incidents of flying tiles, missing letters, and dropped SCRABBLE boards.

We learned two key things going forward. Generally, kids under ten years old were simply too young. And for School SCRABBLE, we should replace the standard SCRABBLE board with the deluxe model, where the tiles are secured in grids.

Numerous trips to middle schools confirmed our thoughts that ages ten to thirteen would be the best participants in School SCRABBLE. That has been the traditional age range for the National Spelling Bee and many school chess programs. Also, kids that age are reasonably socialized but not too jaded.

One of our first field trips was to a middle school in Springfield. The kids took to the game almost immediately—well over half of them saying they'd played it at home. There were a lot of high fives, word challenges, and light trash talk. The teacher could not believe how engaged her students were. She uttered the phrase I'd hear numerous times in ensuing years: "They're learning and they don't even know it!" Exactly. She later wrote us and said she was using SCRABBLE as an incentive. "I told them if they finished the lesson plan early, they could play SCRABBLE. I never saw them so motivated."

Trips to other middle schools yielded identical results, regardless of the location or composition of the class. Inspired by the experience, we developed materials geared specifically for the kids. "Cool Words to Know" was the two- and three-letter words, Q-without-U words, common JQXZ words, and more. Another piece, understandably popular, was "How to Beat Your Parents at SCRABBLE."

We developed materials for teachers as well. Our NSA School SCRABBLE Program director, Yvonne Lieblein, worked with NSA players Ben Greenwood and Christine Economos, who were teachers and educational consultants, to this end. First, they created key vocabulary exercises using the SCRABBLE board and tiles. Then they created lesson plans based directly on state and nationally mandated vocabulary guidelines, as well as a series of SCRABBLE-based activity books to be sold at retail.

Another key contributor was Dr. Paul Folkemer of the Benjamin Franklin Middle School in Ridgewood, New Jersey. Dr. Folkemer was a past National Middle School Principal of the Year and a true SCRABBLE fanatic. In fact, he'd created a daily SCRABBLE challenge that was telecast on his school's classroom network. The daily feature was picked up by a local cable access channel, and soon the whole town was playing along with the kids!

On an early visit to Benjamin Franklin Middle School, it had been arranged for me to play five games at once against five teams of two students each. At least one of those teams beat me as I scurried back and forth trying to make my best plays. In one key game, I was about to lose when I saw the seven-letter play POOPERS on my rack.

I was so focused that my only thought was "party poopers." Swear to God. So I laid the tiles down against my opponents, a pair of eleven-year-old boys. You can imagine their reaction to seeing the word POOPERS—and then the reaction of the boys next to them, then the rest of the class, then the dismayed teacher. Muffled by giggles and hoots of laughter, I tried in vain to explain the word, but the damage had been done. Only later did I learn that the word POOPERS was not a legal word in SCRABBLE, regardless of its meaning.

Our research visits to high schools proved less fruitful. In fact, we cut these short because it was apparent early on that SCRABBLE in the classroom or as an extracurricular activity just wasn't optimal for this demographic. The reasons were numerous. High school students are already overbooked, and even the most enticing SCRABBLE scenarios were no match for raging hormones. Almost every game we tried at the high school level became an opportunity for flirting, teasing, and goofing around. I remember vainly trying to explain the joy of playing an obscure word to a noisy, distracted group of Long Island teenagers. As I trudged back from the front of the classroom to join my colleagues, a sullen fifteen-year-old boy glared at me. "Dork," he muttered.

▪ ▪ ▪

When our field work was completed in 1992, it was time to both announce and launch the National School SCRABBLE Program. It was clear that we had two key needs: a partner to help us get into schools, and materials.

For the partner, we chose Scholastic, the venerable and highly respected educational publisher, which had a division specifically charged with this kind of mission—to help companies responsibly and realistically introduce viable new products to schools. Scholastic had the experience, credibility, and database we needed. As a team, we all began work on a direct-mail piece introducing School SCRABBLE and its educational benefits. As we'd done so often before, the NSA recommended that the Hasbro name be minimized in the endeavor; make it about the game.

For the second element, the NSA created a School SCRABBLE Kit. The idea was to have everything necessary for a classroom of twenty-four students contained in one box. We recommended the following materials be included: six SCRABBLE games with the raised grid surface, racks, tiles, an *Official SCRABBLE Players Dictionary*, the "Cool Words to Know" word list to be photocopied, a curriculum guide for the teacher, and a five-minute video showing a classroom full of cool middle school kids having the time of their lives playing SCRABBLE.

I'll skip over the year-by-year growth of the program and simply say that it was a huge success by any standard. After a successful launch, we went on to sell more than thirty thousand kits in the next decade with over a million students participating.

We learned so much. One of the significant findings was that, at the end of the day, any endeavor is only as good as its local operatives. This holds true whether it's a Scout troop, 4-H club, chess club, or gymnastics club. We came to appreciate how much pressure is on teachers from so many sources: parents, the administration, the state educational offices, and the students themselves. We also learned that many teachers bought School SCRABBLE Kits with their own money or from a small classroom budget rather than send the request through a labyrinth of financial approvals.

This launch also gave me a personal reality check in regard to dealing with a couple of large organizations. The National PTA, which I assumed would be a natural partner, was a complete dead end. A trip to their annual convention indicated to me that they were more about fund-raising than about curriculum. This led us to create a brochure on how to use SCRABBLE as a fund-raiser; one of the chief ways was to have people pledge money for points scored during a tournament. While the PTA never embraced this, we did have more luck with the Literacy Volunteers of America and its successor, ProLiteracy Worldwide. These groups stage up to seventy-five SCRABBLE-themed fund-raisers a year throughout North America and by late 2013 had raised nearly $2 million doing this.

My most disappointing institutional encounter was with the Department of Education (DOE) in Washington. I had called the office of my congressman in the House of Representatives. They gave me a contact name at the DOE, whom I called six times without a return phone call. On the first call, I simply left my name and a fifteen-word message. On the third phone call, I left a longer message. I emphasized that we were not looking for funding, an endorsement, or even a meeting. All we wanted was to know if in their myriad platforms for communicating with the nation's schools, there might be a place to mention this innovative new teaching idea. On the sixth call, I left a brief message: that I was no longer interested in the DOE's help, but was curious as to the magic number of phone calls needed before someone called me back. That went unanswered as well.

Another huge School SCRABBLE disappointment was my

dealings with Electronic Arts (EA), who held the license from Hasbro for the SCRABBLE Internet and Digital rights in North America. The NSA worked with them when they first acquired the rights, consulting on marketing and development of the online game. The executives I dealt with were fun, delightful people, but I concluded they were mostly interested in having "Endorsed by the National SCRABBLE Association" on their products.

Early on, I had urged both Hasbro and EA to take ownership of kids' SCRABBLE play on the Internet. In 2004, we suggested a plan to form online School SCRABBLE Clubs with proctored interclub play and individual play between members. I felt this was critical to the health—hell, survival—of the brand for the future. Imagine a middle school in Florida challenging a middle school in Illinois to a match!

EA agreed this was a great idea and authorized me to go on national television to announce it. So during an ESPN telecast of the National School SCRABBLE Championship—more on that later—I appeared, gushing about the development of this idea. Embarrassingly, it never happened. Unfortunately, as I write this, there is still no designated place for kids to play SCRABBLE with other kids or schools on the Internet. Most serious School SCRABBLE players have found their way either to Words with Friends or to an illegal site run out of Romania.

From the very beginning of School SCRABBLE, we had talked about eventually having a National School SCRABBLE Championship (NSSC). This was inspired by the National Spelling Bee as well as our own National SCRABBLE Championship for adults. Competitions of this kind were beginning to flourish. In addition to the spelling bee, there were national vocabulary, geography, and math "bees" as well. Of course, the leader in all this was chess. School chess programs and competition have been thriving forever. This is pretty astonishing, given chess's learning curve and intellectually intimidating reputation.

Despite the lack of an official Internet school and kids' platform to help drive our efforts, the School SCRABBLE Program continued to grow—especially in terms of competition. So as we contemplated our first national event, we began with a couple of tournaments in Massachusetts, then a New England–wide tournament in Boston in 2001.

We learned a lot along the way. For openers, less is more. So rather than go with the adult tournament time limit of twenty-five total minutes, we kept the kids at twenty-two minutes per team. We also learned that kids bring a lot of playground behavior indoors for this sort of thing. There was a lot of teasing and trash-talking—to the point we had to establish a Sportsmanship Award to deter this.

Of course, there was a wide range of types of kids, skill levels, and hijinks. At one tournament, we had a pair of seventh-grade girls who realized their fifth-grade boy opponents were complete novices. Midway into the game, they decided to start laying random, absurd combinations of letters on the board. Their plays might have included nonwords such as GRUNK, MARP, and BANBAY. The boys were too intimidated to challenge and deferred on every play, so the girls won by hundreds of points. Needless to say, this particular girls' team did not win the Sportsmanship Award. In fact, because of this, we changed the rules to put a ceiling on the margin of victory a team could achieve.

One classic tournament sight was a game between two

eighth-grade girls and, again, a pair of fifth-grade boys. This time, the boys were from an all-male Catholic school. They sat stick straight, side by side, in starched white shirts, school ties, and blazers with the school crest.

The girls were another story. We all know the differences in physical maturity between a thirteen-year-old girl and a ten-year-old boy. So suffice it to say these two girls were light-years ahead of these two boys in the puberty sweepstakes. And their fashion sense had a touch more flair than that found at a typical Catholic school. Inspired by, perhaps, Britney Spears, each girl was fully made up, bejeweled, and confident.

Each time I walked by their table, the boys were doing one of two things. They either stared straight ahead, silently watching as the girls frolicked across from them, or they kept their heads down, eyes averted, as these apprentice sirens cast their spell over the board. I never did find out who won that game.

Another thing we learned was that every year the level of play became better and better. Sure, there were always newbies in the back of the room—and we embraced them—but the kids at the leading tables were becoming as good as some adult tournament players. There were numerous reasons for that. Sometimes parents, recognizing a new interest, brought the kids to a local adult SCRABBLE club for competition and pointers. Books such as *Word Freak* and *Everything SCRABBLE®* told about the joy of the game and offered tips and exercises. And there were now schools that'd been using School SCRABBLE for a number of years, so the second and third round of students were more advanced.

We went on to have our first National School SCRABBLE

Championship in Boston in 2003, spearheaded locally by SCRABBLE promoter Sherrie Saint John and her husband, Gregg Foster. From there, we held them in Providence, Orlando, and Washington, DC. Although the event was still held on the East Coast, we were starting to go national for competitors. From the early New England–only players, we now had kids from California, Texas, Indiana, North Carolina, Utah, Oregon, Canada, and more. Hasbro continued to support the NSA with a beautiful hotel site, thousand of dollars in prize money, an opening reception, breakfast and lunch, trophies, and welcome packages with games, T-shirts, and other goodies for students and coaches. Our friends at Merriam-Webster donated free SCRABBLE dictionaries and created an annual word-based contest with a substantial prize such as an iPad.

Below is an example of the contest for the kids for the 2012 NSSC. Let's see how well you can do against the young word wizards who entered.

Use Your Merriam-Webster
Official SCRABBLE Players Dictionary, Fourth Edition
to Score High
Spell it out for a chance to win a Kindle Touch
3G e-reader from Merriam-Webster!

A blue color (*adjective*) 10 points _ _ _ _ _ _ _ _
To gossip (*verb*) 24 points _ _ _ _ _ _ _ _
Standard keyboard (*noun*) 21 points _ _ _ _ _ _
Extremely idealistic (*adjective*) 26 points _ _ _ _ _ _ _ _

To seize a vehicle while in transit (*verb*) 22 points _ _ _ _
_ _

A cell formed by the union of two gametes (*noun*) 19
points _ _ _ _ _ _

To cover with a thin varnish (*verb*) 12 points _ _ _ _ _ _ _

The science that deals with animals (*noun*) 20 points _ _
_ _ _ _ _

A question (*noun*) 19 points _ _ _ _ _ _ _

A marketplace (*noun*) 17 points _ _ _ _ _ _

Answers on page 203.

Although the events were fully funded, it's important to note that every team paid its own way to the National School SCRABBLE Championship. The typical contingent from a school would be two kids, a coach, two parents, and a handful of siblings, so there was a fair amount of money involved. Sometimes teams were underwritten by a PTA or school activities budget. Often the school would hold bake sales or a car wash to raise the necessary funds.

It was inspirational to see schools, classmates, and the community getting behind this mission. In many areas, the NSSC competitors were considered as important as any athletic team headed off to a big tournament. One of the coolest scenarios was when a winning school returned home to a rally in which the National School SCRABBLE Championship silver cup was placed in the school's trophy case along with those of the football, baseball, and gymnastic teams!

This played to our core message to the kids: that you could

get recognition, travel, win money, and take part in serious competition even if you could not run fast, jump high, or throw a ball with accuracy. Hey, if I can convince one kid that Smart Is Cool, I will have justified my time on earth.

So by 2009, the National School SCRABBLE Championship had grown to the point that first prize was $10,000 for the winning team. Even better, we were about to make both the kids and adult experts TV stars!

The SCRABBLE 50th Anniversary Celebrity SCRABBLE Tournament at Madison Square Garden in New York, March 1998. Former *Saturday Night Live* star and current U.S. senator Al Franken and his partner, NBA Hall of Fame player Walt "Clyde" Frazier, plot their next move. *(Marty Heitner photo)*

One of the early prototypes of SCRABBLE from the 1930s. Note the architect's paper used by the game's inventor, Alfred Mosher Butts. Also note on the left that the game was still called Criss Cross Words at the time. *(Marty Heitner photo/Alfred Butts Estate)*

SCRABBLE inventor Alfred Mosher Butts in a publicity shot circa 1980. A brilliant, creative, and humble man, he admitted he was astonished by the worldwide success of his idea. It's estimated over 100 million SCRABBLE sets have been sold. *(Selchow & Righter photo)*

The late Rita Norr with John D. Williams Jr. in 1987, moments after she became the only woman in history to win the National SCRABBLE Championship. This photograph was taken at the Sahara Hotel in Las Vegas. It turned out that Rita and John owned houses barely a mile apart on eastern Long Island, more than two thousand miles away, where they played a match three days later.

MULLIGATAWNY—one of the most famous SCRABBLE moves of all time. It was played by the late Joe Simpson against his friend Fred Smedley at the legendary Washington Square Park SCRABBLE scene in New York. Fred opened with TAWNY. Joe studied his rack and found MULLIGA. Fred challenged, and they had to walk to Joe's nearby apartment for a dictionary that contained the word! Mulligatawny is a rich soup seasoned with curry. *(Patty Hocker photo)*

MILTON BRADLEY CO.

GAMES

Card and Paper Trimmers
School and Kindergarten Material

Cable-
MILTBRADCO

Springfield, Mass.

November 15, 1933

Mr. Alfred M. Butts
101 Park Avenue
New York City

Dear Sir:

     After giving your game our very careful review and
consideration, we do not feel we would be interested in adding
this item to our line.

     We are returning the model under separate cover.

     Very truly yours,

     MILTON BRADLEY COMPANY

     George A. Fox

     Manager Game Department

:S

Thanks, but no thanks. Here's a 1933 letter from game manufacturer Milton Bradley to Alfred Mosher Butts rejecting his submission of an early version of SCRABBLE. *(Marty Heitner photo/Alfred Butts Estate)*

The largest National SCRABBLE Championship in history, with over 840 contestants playing for the $25,000 top prize. Trey Wright defeated SCRABBLE National, ALL*STARS, and Superstars Showdown champion David Gibson for the 2004 title in New Orleans. *(Patty Hocker photo)*

Highest game score ever! Mike Cresta defeated Wayne Yorra 830–490 in the highest-scoring official game in history at the Lexington, Massachusetts, club on October 12, 2006. Cresta's 830 points eradicated the previous record of 770 points held by California's Mark Landsberg, and the combined 1,320 points shattered the previous mark by almost 200 points. Among the high-scoring plays: JOUSTED, LADYLIKE, FLATFISH, UNDERDOG, SCAMSTER, and QUIXOTRY. Astonishingly, neither player is a tournament expert. *(Patty Hocker photo)*

Parker Brothers
INCORPORATED
Manufacturers of

Games

Salem, Mass., U.S.A.

GRAND PRIZE AND GOLD MEDAL
WORLD'S FAIR
SAINT LOUIS, 1904
HIGHEST AWARD
WORLD'S COLUMBIAN EXPOSITION
CHICAGO 1893

NEW YORK
FLATIRON BUILDING
LONDON: 12 WHITELEY ROAD
CABLE ADDRESS
"PARKER SALEM"
WESTERN UNION CODE

October 17, 1934

Mr. Alfred M. Butts,
101 Park Ave.,
New York City

Dear Sir:

    Our New Games Committee has carefully considered the game which you so kindly sent in to us for examination. While the game no doubt contains considerable merit, we do not feel that it is adaptable to our line.

    The games we have planned and developed far in advance, make a very attractive addition to our line, and are quite sufficient under present conditions. Therefore, we are returning your material to you, under separate cover.

    We thank you sincerely for your kindness and courtesy in writing to us, and hope that you will remember us when you think of games.

        Very truly yours,

        PARKER BROTHERS (INC.)

        L. R. Howard
        Development Manager

LRH;FGT

    P.S. Of course, you know, you are invited to send in any other ideas for games that may occur to you. All games submitted will be for 1935 consideration.

Thanks, but no thanks (part 2). Here's a 1934 letter from game manufacturer Parker Brothers to Alfred Mosher Butts rejecting his submission of an early version of SCRABBLE. Somebody goofed. *(Marty Heitner photo/Alfred Butts Estate)*

SCRABBLE inventor Alfred Mosher Butts, pictured here
fifty years after inventing the classic word game. Previous
game owner Selchow & Righter uncovered a second game
he'd constructed and named it Alfred's Other Game.
Positioned as a solitaire version of SCRABBLE, it was
launched in the mid–1980s but never really took off.
Someone at the company's advertising agency thought
it would be a good idea to do a James Bond–inspired
photograph for the marketing campaign.

10

SCHOOL SCRABBLE
MAKES THE GRADE

I T TOOK A COUPLE OF YEARS, but we were able to grow the National School SCRABBLE Championship into a truly spectacular event. The best part is that it grew in every way. More kids participated. The student competitors continued to catch up with adults in their abilities, and the world was starting to pay more attention to our core messages: it's cool to be smart, and competition can take many forms. As a bonus, it was proven that the world's favorite word game could enrich lives and help teach in unanticipated ways.

Our efforts reached their high point around 2010. The glint of an idea a decade or so earlier had gone from a small ballroom at the Marriott in Springfield, Massachusetts, Royal Pacific Resort in family-friendly Orlando.

By now, the event had become a family affair. It was routine to see a young competitor accompanied by as many as a half-dozen relatives—most of whom would sit patiently on the sidelines during play, even though they really couldn't see any "action." Team uniforms had also become standard. Scores of colorfully decorated T-shirts, baseball caps, and hoodies bore the name—or nickname—of each team. Examples might include the Word Wizards, the Tile Masters, or the clever You Can't Spell Awesome Without Me!

The NSA's Jane Ratsey Williams and staff also organized a wondrous evening social to build camaraderie and relax the competitors a bit. It was always a themed party, once a luau with leis for each guest, another time a Cinco de Mayo party complete with a mariachi band. We'd serve up plenty of treats for the students and their families, with ice cream sundaes, fruit parfaits for kids with allergies, and a fun take-home memento. Another highlight of the party would be games. It was fun to see these kids—after a day of intense matches of SCRABBLE—playing other classics such as Jenga, Scattergories, Perfection, Twister, and Boggle. To add to the excitement we also made sure to have on hand a couple of adult National SCRABBLE Champions—who are heroes to kids—to play fun matches against groups of youngsters. These events emphasized and reinforced the beauty of board games. Children from North Carolina would be playing Monopoly with kids from Toronto. Thirteen-year-old girls would be competing, and practicing flirting, against two brothers from Texas.

As you might imagine, Hasbro executives almost wept with appreciation as they witnessed this swirl of two hundred kids and their families captivated by their products. After all, this was not a Saturday morning commercial on Nickelodeon with child actors; this was the real deal. It was important for all of us involved to make this event the experience of a lifetime for everyone who attended—whether it was the team who won $10,000 or the fifth-grade first-timers who lost almost every game. As in sports, the life lessons learned from games are invaluable and incalculable.

Then there was the actual competition. The skill level of some middle school students had become so refined and lethal that they now routinely played and defeated grown-ups in official play.

This evolution was hammered home in dramatic fashion at the 2008 National SCRABBLE Championship in Orlando. Remember, this is arguably the largest and toughest SCRABBLE tournament in the world, and that year it featured $100,000 in cash prizes. It included twenty-eight intense games over five days. Players competed in six divisions, depending on their skill level and rating. Astonishingly, four of the six divisions were won by kids coming out of the School SCRABBLE Program, the oldest being just twenty years old. If we'd ever had any doubts about the ability of the program to feed the tournament scene, they were eradicated by those performances.

The National School SCRABBLE Championship remains one of the most meaningful, exhausting, and fun experiences of my life—on both a professional and personal level. I'll never forget getting to know these young champions and their families. All of us at the NSA and the people from Hasbro Games also gleaned enormous satisfaction from watching the kids go through this experience.

While the championship is the high-profile centerpiece of the National School SCRABBLE Program, it's important to pay tribute to what is happening on the local level throughout the country. In Washington, DC, for example, we went from no presence whatsoever to having a School SCRABBLE club in every single middle school in the city—127 in all. Spearheaded by DC resident Stefan Fatsis and, on the NSA side, Jane Ratsey Williams and Katie Schulz Hukill, the Washington initiative became a true template of what we were trying to do all over the country. It typically began with a visit to a school, or a conference with teachers or administrators from many schools. Most meetings began with us showing a fun, energetic video of kids playing SCRABBLE. Next came explanations about the School SCRABBLE Kit, educational benefits, program guidelines, and game rules, and random questions.

As with anything of this nature, the growth was organic. That said, once SCRABBLE was introduced properly into a classroom or as an after-school activity, the rest took care of itself. After all, SCRABBLE is nothing if not approachable for kids. The rules are simple, and there is plenty of scoring. Time and again, we witnessed the sense of discovery when students "got it." Just like generations before them who'd learned about the game around the kitchen table, these kids couldn't get enough of it.

Philadelphia became another hotspot for kids and SCRABBLE. The driving force there was Marciene Mattleman, a dynamo who seemed to know everyone in the City of Brotherly Love. Marciene is a longtime media personality and social activist, the kind of individual who is unwilling to take no for an answer. She and her organization, the Philadelphia After School Activities Partnerships (ASAP), had earlier success with a vigorous after-school program featuring chess. Now it was SCRABBLE's turn, and Marciene took it city-wide. Marciene, who coincidentally knew Stefan Fatsis from his days at Penn and as a young reporter, soon brought impressive participation to Philadelphia's School SCRABBLE effort as well. By 2012, Philadelphia had annual school championships, more than a hundred clubs, and thousands of kids involved. Marciene also cajoled numerous mayors, politicians, and business leaders to both attend and contribute to the effort. Throughout this, Marciene was fortunate enough to work with NSA member Matt Hopkins, a local SCRABBLE organizer and one of the most respected people in the NSA community.

Chicago was a different story. As noted, outreach is only as good as one's local contact and operatives. In the Windy City, that turned out to be not an educational institution but the Chicago-based American Library Association via our main contact, Jenny Levine. Jenny's another hardworking, smart, caring person who believes in the greater good and has chosen the not-for-profit career to the benefit of all of us. She also introduced us to having a presence at both the American Library Association National Conferences and the Public Library Association. Working closely together, we were able to establish nearly eight hundred library SCRABBLE clubs across the United States for kids and families.

As clubs started sprouting up outside of traditional schools and libraries, we noticed that SCRABBLE clubs were also starting to sprout up in other unanticipated venues such as Scouts and 4-H clubs. To expand this outreach, NSA staff members started to attend various annual conventions to spread the word: middle school teachers, gifted and talented programs, the Girl Scouts of America, the National Reading Association, Newspapers in Education, the National PTA, and others.

Each conference taught us something new. We learned that education was a multilayered entity and a big business. It was also no place for idealists. Though we bore the warm and fuzzy banner of America's beloved word game—along with an innovative teaching approach—we were subjected to the same gauntlet of skepticism, testing, waiting, and approval as anyone else. Everyone wants to do business with schools because it's an important and feel-good enterprise, but there is also a lot of money to be made. And, understandably, everyone has a voice: federal and state government, school boards, parents, and teachers. So we had to become realists with a lot of patience

Having grown up just thirty miles from New York City, I was especially excited about taking on Gotham on behalf of School SCRABBLE. We went at this a couple of ways. First, we have a mutual friend with Caroline Kennedy Schlossberg, who had become very active as a volunteer to Mayor Michael Bloomberg in an effort to improve the public school system. So we reached out to her, but our timing was bad. Ms. Schlossberg was considering her first attempt at elected politics, possibly running for the US Senate from New York. She later was appointed ambassador to Japan.

Our next plan was to reconnect with legendary New York restaurateur Danny Meyer. One of the nation's most admired businessmen, Danny made his mark with such New York establishments as the Union Square Café, the Gramercy Tavern, the Modern, Blue Smoke, and the Shake Shack franchises, among other ventures. A true SCRABBLE fan, Danny participated in our 1998 SCRABBLE 50th Anniversary SPELL-A-BRATION tournament at Madison Square Garden to benefit literacy. Other guests included Al Franken, Walt "Clyde" Frazier, literacy activist and actress Tina Louise, Miss America, *New York Post* columnist Richard Johnson, and film critic Jeffrey Lyons.

Danny Meyer is known as a caring member of the community and has been involved in numerous charitable causes over the years. So the NSA staff met with Danny and his people and created a project model we felt would work well for New York City and could then be applied to other major markets as well.

The plan was simple. Through Danny Meyer's Union Square Hospitality Group, we would reach out to various restaurants throughout the city. We would then encourage restaurants to purchase one or more School SCRABBLE Kits and donate them to middle schools in their neighborhoods. It would be as little as $49.95 to participate and a great public relations move by participating restaurants.

In addition to this involvement, Danny offered other support. For openers, he would host an event at one of his establishments where we would announce the initiative to the media. Danny also owned one of the city's most desirable Rolodexes, and he offered to invite numerous power brokers, celebrities and others to the event. Understandably, we were thrilled with Danny Meyer's graciousness and potential involvement.

Unfortunately, this is as far as it ever went. The timing was horrible in regard to Hasbro's participation. The NSA was in the throes of dealing with, in my opinion, the least imaginative and least cooperative team of Hasbro Games marketing executives in our twenty-five-year relationship. It got so bad that, despite our efforts, we went *an entire year* without a single face-to-face meeting with anyone at Hasbro! Meanwhile, the Danny Meyer ship had sailed. I suspect he was understandably astonished—and possibly insulted—by our inability to step up and pull the trigger on a project of this scope and importance. I sure was.

Fortunately, we eventually found our way to the New York City Parks and Recreation Department. Even by municipal standards, the Parks and Recreation Department was a vast and deep operation. Among their responsibilities was the organization and supervision of various youth programs in the city's five boroughs.

The Parks people loved the idea of SCRABBLE. They had more than enough of the standard indoor and outdoor activities, and we represented a fresh idea. Plus, the prospect of Hasbro donating School SCRABBLE Kits had great appeal for the schools' cash-strapped budgets.

After our initial meetings with the coordinator, we began a plan to set up SCRABBLE activities at selected locations throughout the city. First the NSA held training sessions with the Parks personnel, just as we had with schoolteachers in Washington, DC, and Philadelphia. Many were unfamiliar with the game and initially intimidated by the prospect. We understood. One of the chief elements of resistance to SCRABBLE—regardless of the venue or group—is that people are afraid that playing will reveal them to be stupid, a terrible speller, or both.

Happily, our effort expanded and even culminated in several local Parks and Recreation tournaments, culminating in a city-wide tournament at the Castle, the headquarters in Central Park. I attended the event and watched the competition with Commissioner Adrian Benepe and his staff. Our goal was to have the winners represent New York City at the next National School SCRABBLE Championship. Unfortunately, as sometimes happens, our initiative lost steam when our main contact left her position, followed by Benepe himself not long thereafter. It's my understanding that this initiative is no longer active.

And then there's Los Angeles. Contrary to what some cynical East Coast intellectuals might assume, LA is one of the most active and successful SCRABBLE cultures in North America. Among its SCRABBLE stars is Roger "Trey" Wright, the 2004

National SCRABBLE Champion and a world-class touring classical pianist. There's also Mark Landsberg, whose record of 770 points scored in an official SCRABBLE match stood for nearly thirteen years. Also in LA were tournament expert and documentary filmmaker Eric Chaikin (*Word Wars*) and Scott Petersen, whose acclaimed *Scrabylon* garnered awards at numerous festivals around the country.

Unfortunately, we never really made any inroads with the LA public school systems or other conventional channels.

11

SCRABBLE HITS TV

O NE OF MY GOALS RUNNING THE NSA was to have an actual SCRABBLE match on television. Chess and poker had been on periodically over the years, and I felt that, done properly, a high-level SCRABBLE match would make for an interesting show. There had been a SCRABBLE game show in the mid-1980s, hosted by the ubiquitous Chuck Woolery. It was actually more like Hangman than SCRABBLE, so, as one might have expected, it was dismissed, if not reviled, by most serious NSA players. The production company even sent two casting people to the 1985 National SCRABBLE Championship to interview "real SCRABBLE experts" to appear on the show. A handful actually made it onto the air, where most got their butts kicked by your average experienced game show contestants.

While we'd had various champions interviewed over the years on television, a broadcast match had remained elusive for us until 2003. We had identified ESPN as our most likely platform for a number of reasons. First, we loved the idea of SCRABBLE being positioned—if not perceived—as a legitimate, serious competitive event. Second, we knew that ESPN was expanding into multiple channels as well as quirky programming such as competitive eating. We saw ourselves fitting right into that niche. After all, it was ESPN that brought the successful National Spelling Bee coverage to national television. It had become such a ratings success that ESPN's broadcast cousin ABC eventually took over the program to expand the audience. Who better to fill in the programming void than SCRABBLE!

Third, we knew that—at the time—one could still essentially buy one's way onto ESPN by buying an hour of time at a negotiated price. After that, the buyer would own the commercials within. In theory, the buyer could then sell off the spots to a third party to offset production and time costs, or use them for itself.

But we were able to go one better. We ultimately convinced ESPN to allot the time at their cost and pay for the production of America's first televised SCRABBLE match.

As it turned out, the NSA was pitching the network from two fronts. My talented colleague and School SCRABBLE Program director, Yvonne Lieblein, had been talking to ESPN executives at their Bristol, Connecticut, headquarters about telecasting the first National School SCRABBLE Championship. I, on the other hand, had been in conversation with veteran ESPN producer and director Jonathan Hock. I met Jon through his best friend, Stefan Fatsis, and we connected over our love of sports, video, and film. Jon is a gifted person, responsible for several programs in ESPN's remarkable *30 for 30* series as well as wonderful documentary work. Jon loved SCRABBLE and was interested in pursuing the project through his own contacts at the network.

I had learned early in my career that very often a particular media outlet might have more than one person chasing down a story. For example, a *New York Times* reporter might be talking to us about a SCRABBLE story while a *Times* columnist might also be thinking of doing a piece. It had happened with NBC, NPR, CNN, and others. I also learned early to simply let the chips fall where they may. It was up to these guys, not me, to decide who was going to do a SCRABBLE piece. They would find out eventually through the editorial process about each other's interest.

At any rate, Yvonne got the call first, and we headed up to ESPN to talk about the project. Jon Hock eventually dropped out. He felt he needed ninety minutes to do the show properly and a larger budget than ESPN was willing to provide.

Our ESPN contacts were friendly, smart, and enthusiastic. However, as we discussed the possibility of the National School SCRABBLE Championship show, I became concerned. The chief reason was that this was going to be the first year of a real *national* school competition—all the others had been regional. There was a plethora of variables and unknowns. How many teams would we have? How good was the level of play? How would the kids—and their parents—behave? As excited as I was to be in the meeting, my gut was telling me that to hold the first-ever NSSC and have it on television at the same time was not a good idea.

So I introduced the idea of having a SCRABBLE All*Stars tournament instead, postponing the NSSC broadcast until at least the following year. It was a concept similar to our 1995 SCRABBLE Superstars Showdown spectacular in Las Vegas. That event generated serious publicity—including a seven-page article in *Sports Illustrated*—and featured the fifty best players in the world vying for $100,000 in cash.

ESPN liked this idea a lot. For openers, it had the built-in all-star sports element. Even better, Hasbro would soon agree to both put up the prize money and underwrite the entire event. ESPN would provide the time and assign an approved producer to the project. They also assigned a designated ESPN person— dynamo Ashley O'Connor Mintz—to be our day-to-day contact.

The ESPN All*Stars event was an astonishing experience for all involved. The NSA staff and Advisory Board worked hard to come up with an eligibility format that was fair. In the end, we decided to invite all former world and national champions, with the rest of the field being eligible by tournament rating. Interestingly, former champions Peter Morris and Brian Cappelletto both emerged from self-imposed retirement for a crack at the $50,000 first prize. While NSA experts often and understandably bemoaned the lack of big prize money compared to chess or poker, this did represent serious progress. After all, not long before, first prize in the National SCRABBLE Championship had been just $5,000.

As expected, the event lived up to its billing in regard to the intensity of the competitors and the level of play. Technically, it was a challenge for the ESPN crew and announcers. These were guys used to filming and talking about nonstop action, and this venue was the opposite. Instead, the play-by-play consisted of words that could have been played, biographical backgrounds of the competitors, and fundamental SCRABBLE tips. For once, I half-wished a few of our more volatile players would start a fistfight or fling a board against the wall. We wanted to deliver viewers bang for their entertainment buck.

Because of time constraints—forty-eight minutes—we knew we were not going to be able to show a SCRABBLE match in its entirety, move by move. The average tournament game takes about forty-five minutes, but we needed time for "up close and personal" player profiles, interviews and commentary, statistics and analysis, etc. So we ended up doing what colleagues everywhere do in the situation. We resolved to shoot as much footage as we could of everything and then figure it all out in postproduction!

The ESPN SCRABBLE All*Stars special featured my most humbling career experience, when I received a standing ovation when I delivered my opening remarks. I knew well that this was a diverse group, many of them ambivalent about me at best. I learned over the years to try not to take it personally. I came to realize that it was not me per se but what I represented. Essentially, I was the person between the business/corporate side of the game and the purist point of view.

As I've mentioned, many players—usually top experts—saw both me and Hasbro as necessary evils who came attached to the game they loved. Worse, the NSA and Hasbro pretty much called the shots as to how the competitive SCRABBLE world was run. We had money, power, and the law on our side. In addition, the players' world was occasionally chaotic, a free-form society with many smart, individualistic, offbeat people wary of authority over *their* game.

Although I'd tried hard to prove myself as a player, I was still an outsider. One of the reasons was that I did not compete regularly in local tournaments or at local SCRABBLE clubs. Part of this was practical. I lived forty-five minutes from the nearest SCRABBLE club. Also, I liked to have weekends for myself. And, although I knew nothing about leadership, I felt it was a good idea not to get too mixed up in the personal lives of NSA members. It would make the job that much more difficult. This is not to say I didn't develop close friends among NSA members. I did, but carefully.

Perhaps the perception of me among players is best summed up in a couple of scenarios. One involves a friend of my family who happened to run across a well-known woman SCRABBLE player at a social event. He's a brilliant young guy, who had defeated me in the very first game we ever played. I remember it well, not only for the personal humiliation but because he had thrown down the word ROADEO against me. I knew damn well it was a guess on his part and challenged.

You know the rest. ROADEO turned out to be an acceptable word, meaning, basically, a rodeo for cars. Who knew! Anyway, he happened to mention the victory to the woman during the conversation, looking for some appreciation or validation. Instead, she immediately scoffed, "So what. John Williams is the *marketing guy.*" He might as well have told her he'd beaten a kindergarten student or a moron.

There was another conversation that epitomized the cluelessness and scorn some top players had for both me and Hasbro. It was a phone call with Floridian Bob Lipton, one of the very top American players for many years.

Lipton and I had enjoyed an ongoing dialogue for a long time, primarily about how I ran the organization and about the NSA policy on new allowable words. He was one of the early proponents of an expanded dictionary for North American play. It was referred to as the SOWPODS list, and it was essentially all the international, or "English," words combined with the existing "American" words. SOWPODS was an anagram of the abbreviated titles of the *Official SCRABBLE Players Dictionary* and England's *Official SCRABBLE Words.*

Lipton was of the more-words-the-merrier faction of tournament players. Not surprisingly, most in this group were top experts and avid studiers of word lists. Words such as ZA and QI—later acceptable here—were just more ammo in their arsenal. But there was one problem. This was a minority vision among NSA members at large.

It was my opinion at the time that most NSA players—and casual players at home—felt there were *too many words* already. Hell, there are four thousand four-letter words alone—many unknown by even midrated tournament SCRABBLE players. Now the SOWPODS group wanted to add another forty thousand more!

Lipton and another proponent, the late veteran expert Stu Goldman, insisted that the NSA mandate that the "international" word list be made official. Not so fast, I countered. I explained that the NSA was going to grow from the bottom up, not from the top down. Thus we really needed to take into account the opinions and wishes of lower-ranked players.

Lipton then asked me a question that left me stunned. It went something like, "Does Hasbro realize that SCRABBLE could disappear and go out of business if these new words are not adopted?"

In my opinion this was a question so mired in myopia and naïveté, I had no immediate answer. But I did have an ultimate answer: democracy. We decided to have the first organization-wide referendum in the history of the NSA in 2000. I felt this was too volatile a topic for the NSA to mandate one set of words over another. Let the players speak.

So we sent out ballots to all members in good standing and asked one question. Did members want the expanded dictionary, or were they happy with things just as they were? When the results were tallied, approximately 67 percent of the NSA membership wanted to stick with things as they were—no international words.

It's important to realize that I had no real opinion in this matter. For me personally, it would just be adding another batch of words I'd never know to the sixty or seventy thousand I already didn't know. But I felt that any change this substantial had to happen organically, and that's what I told Lipton and other SOWPODS adherents. To me, it was no different from the three-point shot becoming acceptable in basketball or the instant-replay review being used for official calls in pro football. It would, I explained, happen over time when, and if, it was meant to happen.

And that is exactly what occurred. In time, interest in the "international game" started to gain momentum, despite the fact that Hasbro had stopped sponsoring the World SCRABBLE Championship in 2001 and Mattel had systematically reduced its funding as well. However, as happened so often in the past, the SCRABBLE subculture rose to the occasion to provide missing elements for the hardcore player.

Previous examples of this include customized boards with superior turntables and personalized graphics or monograms. There were also customized tile bags, customized chess clocks, elongated racks, unlicensed books and study materials, limited-edition T-shirts, and more.

Anyway, interest in international play—and its accompanying dictionary—slowly began to build as the twenty-first century dawned. This was despite both manufacturers losing interest in funding the World SCRABBLE Championship. There were myriad reasons for this. First, as with everything else in our lives, the Internet made a huge difference. Though mostly on illegal sites, you could now find a SCRABBLE opponent any time of day, anywhere in the world, of matching skill and preference in word authority. It was no longer necessary to tour Europe or be among the handful of competitors in a World SCRABBLE Championship to play the international game.

The landscape in learning new words had changed greatly, too, also due to technology. Gone were the days when players used to covet secret word lists, painstakingly researched and compiled the old-fashioned way—word by word. Now you could almost customize your study habits with a push of a keyboard button. For example, let's say I recognize that I have a weakness in five-letter words ending in CH. Don't laugh; it gets this precise and then some. I can find that list somewhere on the Internet, or create it myself, in a format that has been proven easy to memorize. Hence, the prospect of learning thousands of new words is not as daunting as it once was.

Ultimately, all this led to growth in the international game. By 2012, it had reached the point where many local tournaments and the National SCRABBLE Championship itself had a separate "Collins Division"—*Collins SCRABBLE Dictionary* being the name of the dictionary published in England by HarperCollins that includes both the American and English acceptable words.

All this is a way of saying the standing ovation from these experts at the SCRABBLE All*Stars event was meaningful. Even one of my biggest critics, perpetually disgruntled expert Marlon Hill, joined in. He had once said something like "John Williams represents everything that is wrong with SCRABBLE."

He also remarked that the game should be on a big-time circuit with players paid to wear Nike footwear and the like. Sadly, that doesn't appear to be happening anytime soon.

Another touching highlight of the event featured two of my favorite experts—Chris Cree from Texas and David Gibson from South Carolina. Chris is a larger-than-life, well-dressed, successful businessman, a Texan in every way. He has been one of the nation's top players for over thirty years and to some extent is my successor, as he—along with John Chew—is copresident of the North American SCRABBLE Players Association, the new governing body of the game in the wake of the 2013 closing of the NSA. More on that later.

Despite Chris Cree's proven skill, he has never been able to win "the big one," that is, a World, National, or All*Stars SCRABBLE Championship. But it appeared he finally might do it at the 2003 SCRABBLE All*Stars. As we approached the finals, Chris and David were paired in a do-or-die game. The winner would go on to the finals of the richest SCRABBLE tournament in history against arguably the strongest field in history. The loser, through the nuances of the pairing system, would automatically drop as low as sixth place.

It should be noted that David Gibson is one of the most unassuming and beloved players in the game. He also belongs in any discussion about the best players in history, having won the 1994 Nationals and the 1995 Superstars in Las Vegas. At the latter tournament, David took his $50,000 first prize, kept less than half for himself, and distributed all the rest among the other competitors! It was a display of sportsmanship and graciousness never seen in the SCRABBLE world before.

So these two longtime friends sat down for the crucial game

at ESPN SCRABBLE All*Stars. The room was thick with anticipation, the stakes astronomical. What happened next is best told by Chris Cree himself.

"So I'm ready to start, but first I look over at David," Chris recalled years later, "and he's crying." Chris knew exactly why. These guys had so much respect and love for each other that they were seriously conflicted about winning.

Chris continued, "So then I start to cry too. We look at each other in silence, then stand up and hug."

I'd noticed what was happening from across the room. By the time I reached the table, they'd progressed from crying to damn near weeping. Each knew one of them was poised for a painful loss at the hands of a close friend.

The three of us made small talk for a minute or two, and then they both jumped up again for another hug and a few more tears. Finally, Chris and David composed themselves and the game began. I too was on the verge of tears from the experience. It spoke so deeply not only about both men but about the complex relationship—in all sports and competition—between friendship and rivalry.

Sadly, the game itself was an anticlimax. David won decisively and went on to win the ESPN SCRABBLE All*Stars Championship, defeating 1985 NSC champion Ron Tiekert. Though admired and well liked by the SCRABBLE community, Ron was clearly not the favorite among the other competitors. For them, a David Gibson victory might mean divvying up the pot once again. And that's exactly what happened.

We spent a couple of months in postproduction cobbling all the footage into a forty-eight-minute telecast. It wasn't easy. Originally, we'd pushed ESPN for a ninety-minute time slot, but the network rarely, if ever, had a ninety-minute show, and they weren't going to do it for SCRABBLE. Our wish to show a complete high-level SCRABBLE game with commentary, as well as some "up close and personal" profiles of various players, was seriously compromised.

Another concern was exposure and promotion for the eventual telecast. It was explained to us early in the project that ESPN does not do a lot of heavy promotion. This was especially true for niche programming, which we were. So while were we able to alert the entire SCRABBLE world about the All*Stars telecast, it was not exactly top-of-mind for either sports fans or television viewers.

That was reflected in the ratings. They were tepid at best, with perhaps a half million people watching at peak viewership. Televised poker had up to five times more viewers. Even the National Spelling Bee had had more than twice our numbers, although they'd had over twenty years to build the franchise. So both the network and we were understandably disappointed, but we had a five-year deal and plenty of time to do it better. And there was a lot of triumph as well. No network in history had ever broadcast a match featuring a branded board game. Dampened expectations aside, we'd achieved our goal of having a SCRABBLE match on national television.

Reviews of the show itself were scarce and mixed at best. The first airing was largely ignored by the press. Opinions among NSA members, however, were plentiful and predictably all over the place. Some wanted more strategy and less glitz. Others felt it played more like a highlight reel given the absence of a true complete game.

Suggestions for improving the next telecast were equally

diverse. One person insisted we should mike the players, even though most SCRABBLE experts rarely mumble more than a few words during a game. A friend said we should take a cue from professional wrestling—give the players theatrical entrances, stage names, and jerseys festooned with numerous sponsor logos.

Perhaps the best suggestion—one we'd come up with ourselves—was to develop some colorful and meaningful graphics to help tell the story and underscore the wondrous subtleties of the game. For example, if a player's rack featured the letters ISP-DOTE, we could immediately flash on the screen all the anagrams of the word: DEPOSIT, DOPIEST, PODITES, POSITED, SOPITED, TOPSIDE. This would be a cool feature for a number of reasons.

First, it would reward the casual SCRABBLE player with words that were familiar. For the more advanced, it would feature some esoteric words. And chances are both parties would learn a new word or two. Another graphic, using the available artificial intelligence, was to illustrate the best play options from a statistical viewpoint. Then we could take those specific words and move them to various spots on the board to illustrate strategy and options.

In our postmortem with both ESPN and Hasbro, we agreed on one thing. Given the growing popularity and ratings of the National Spelling Bee and our positive experience at our first National School SCRABBLE Championship, it was definitely time to put the kids on television.

12

GOING HOLLYWOOD

AMONG THE LESSONS I'VE LEARNED IN dealing with Hollywood is that you are as good as anyone needs you at any given time. After that, no guarantees. This was absolutely hammered home to me during an experience I had back in 2000. I received a call from an LA-based production executive regarding the use of SCRABBLE in a proposed Jennifer Lopez movie, *The Wedding Planner.*

I should start off by saying that the movie was a big hit despite tepid reviews that saw it as another paint-by-numbers romantic comedy. The project, which also starred Matthew McConaughey, was a classic example of why major studios will always invest in a big star with a mediocre script as opposed to a great script with an unknown actor. It's a business decision: go with a sure thing.

I received this call a few weeks before shooting was about to begin. I'd already known about the project because a year earlier I'd read the screenplay for Hasbro to make sure that SCRABBLE was portrayed accurately and that there was no prurient content or violence involving a SCRABBLE board, tiles, or other icons of the game.

Arguably playing against type, Jennifer Lopez had been cast as a SCRABBLE tournament player and devoted attendee at a SCRABBLE club in San Francisco. The script contained a few scenes involving the game. One was at the SCRABBLE club and another at an important championship, where JLo was poised to win both the competition and Matthew McConaughey's heart.

During the conversation with the production person, I had to explain that I found a few erroneous assumptions made by the screenwriters. First, no NSA tournament ever had four people playing the same game. It was always one-on-one. Second, other than Jennifer Lopez, every SCRABBLE player in the script seemed to be depicted as either a white-haired senior citizen or a crazed geek just this side of the Unabomber. Third, no tournament final ever took place on a stage with an audience of hundreds just twenty-five feet away, as written.

The executive listened patiently to my comments. Authenticity, he assured me, was "the key to the movie's soul." Taking this cue, I then explained such NSA tournament staples as chess clocks, tracking sheets, customized tile bags and racks, and more. As the conversation wound down, he asked me if I would be available to serve as the SCRABBLE technical adviser on the film.

It goes without saying I agreed. In fact, I spent the ensuing weeks extrapolating that upcoming gig in my imagination. It included the first-class flight to LA and a hotel suite down the road from the studio. Then there were the SCRABBLE lessons with JLo between takes and drinks with my soon-to-be main man Matt McConaughey, in which I'd impart some fresh perspective on the script's characters. And, though my participation was already underwritten by Hasbro as part of my job, I'd most likely get a hefty check from grateful producers after my work was done.

So after we hung up, I wrote a long memo outlining my suggestions as discussed. The NSA also sent along boxes of supplies, signage, games, tiles, and dictionaries. Then I sat back and waited for the phone calls about arrangements or questions from JLo and other actors about their character's motivation and the like. Before long, some Hasbro execs and NSA members started referring to "the Jennifer Lopez SCRABBLE movie."

Weeks passed. Months passed. The phone calls never came. Eventually, the movie opened. I happened to catch an interview between JLo and Rosie O'Donnell in which they both gushed about their passion for SCRABBLE. I ended up seeing *The Wedding Planner* a couple of weeks after it had been mostly trashed by critics and NSA members. Still, I walked into a Manhattan movie theater with a relatively open mind.

That didn't last long. I knew we were in trouble when the first scene at the San Francisco SCRABBLE club portrayed the average member's age as between eighty and death. Then there was the scene where JLo reluctantly tells her new love interest that she's a member of the local SCRABBLE group and plays in tournaments. Her character searches his face as he absorbs this revelation.

"Pretty pathetic, huh?" she adds, hoping she hasn't permanently alienated him with this disclosure.

Overall, I'd guess the world's favorite word game was featured for perhaps ten minutes in the two-hour movie. Still, as the credits rolled, I optimistically stayed until the very end. At least I'd see my name mentioned as technical adviser. When that never materialized, I waited to see my name nestled in the general thank-yous at the very end along with the caterers, the mayor's office, and the pet handlers.

Nope. You can bet when they come to me for help with the sequel, I'm really going to give them a piece of my mind.

MARTHA STEWART

For a number of years in the American culture, nothing surpassed an endorsement from Martha Stewart as—to use her famous phrase—"a good thing." So you can imagine my excitement when we arranged for an entire episode of her hit show to be devoted to SCRABBLE. I'd known for a couple of years from media accounts that Martha was a huge fan and very competitive, with a SCRABBLE board in each of her homes.

So an NSA contingent and I headed up to Westport, Connecticut, for the appearance. We'd also arranged for National and World SCRABBLE Champion Brian Cappelletto to fly in from Chicago. Between us, Brian and I would review SCRABBLE fundamentals with Martha in two separate segments. The producers told us that Martha was especially excited about our visit, as were NSA members and Hasbro.

The afternoon before we taped, I was backstage assembling all our props when Martha wandered through and stopped. "You must be the SCRABBLE man," she said. I allowed that I was.

The first thing that struck me was Martha's appearance. She is taller than I expected and has an athlete's build. Not surprisingly, she exudes confidence, an understandable guardedness, and a heard-it-all-before weariness. As it turned out, I was standing in front of a large blown-up photograph of one of her beloved Chow Chow dogs. Trying to find common ground, I mentioned that I had a black half Chow Chow that looked very much like hers. The conversation ground to a halt when she told me that particular dog had recently died.

We were working in a part of the Martha Stewart empire that was a beautiful old house in a residential neighborhood in exclusive Westport. Attached to the house was a sleek state-of-the-art television studio that was completely hidden from the road. The entire staff and production team seemed to be young, hip, and well dressed. They were also very efficient. Most of them commuted from Manhattan, seventy-five miles away, and ate meals prepared in the studio's vast and gleaming kitchen. No surprise there. It was clear that Martha ran a tight ship.

Apparently, however, Martha was much less structured on the air. Right before the segment, the director called me aside.

"We need your help here," he began. "Martha is so smart and has so many ideas—her mind never stops. Because of this, she has a tendency to drift from our script or outline."

I was starting to get concerned as he continued. "So you and I have to review it now, and we need you to drive the spot."

"How exactly am I going to do that?"

"If she starts to go off message, reel her back in. Make her stick to the plan."

Now I was getting nervous.

As it turned out, Martha was great. She's so damned smart, and her SCRABBLE questions were original and incisive. Though we've never played a game, it's clear she understands SCRABBLE strategy very well. The piece came out even better than we anticipated. It's still on YouTube today!

With the exception of a couple of Christmas cards, that was the last interaction I had with Martha Stewart until years later. We reconnected along with some others on a conference call for a proposed project. At one point in the conversation, Martha interrupted and said, "John, you'd be very proud of me. Since I last saw you, I've had time to play a lot of SCRABBLE lately and have learned many new words and gotten a lot better." She was laughing at herself, referring to her recently completed time in prison. We all laughed as well.

JACK BLACK

I've had the good fortune to meet many famous and accomplished people because of my job as NSA executive director. Perhaps my most rewarding encounter was a brief one with the extraordinary actor and musician Jack Black. Like other celebrities, Jack had mentioned his SCRABBLE passion in numerous media stories over the years.

Meeting Jack was a completely serendipitous experience. I was staying in Manhattan at the apartment of film critic Jeffrey Lyons and his wife, Judy, our close family friends. Jeffrey casually mentioned he was going to interview Jack Black the next morning during his regular slot on WNBC. Explaining that the actor was a huge SCRABBLE enthusiast, I asked if I could tag along. Jeffrey said sure.

When we arrived at the studio, Jeffrey sent me to wait in the greenroom, where I encountered a producer who was not happy that I was there. She was understandably protective of the show's guests and indicated it was not a venue for "fans" to meet celebrities. I apologized and said nothing else.

Just as we finished our awkward exchange, Jack Black walked down the hallway with his agent, publicist, and assistant and Jeffrey Lyons. The production woman shot me a quick scowl and quickly positioned herself between me and Jack.

Then Jeffrey spoke. "Jack, I'd like you to meet my good friend John Williams from the National SCRABBLE Assoc—"

Jack Black's usual animated face became ever more animated. "John Williams! Oh, my God. Your book *Everything SCRABBLE*® is like my *Bible*!" Jack turned to the group. "He not only runs the SCRABBLE Association, he's a great player in his own right."

It goes without saying I was feeling pretty good about this. I turned to the production woman, whose facial expression was somewhere between mortified and livid. I didn't have to say a word. Instead, Jack Black looked directly at her and spoke. "Is it okay if John comes out on the set with us? I'd like to talk SCRABBLE with him while we wait to go on the air."

She avoided my gaze completely. "Of course," she said with newfound enthusiasm.

13

JIMMY KIMMEL SPELLS IT OUT

ITHOUT QUESTION, OUR MOST MEANINGFUL HOLLYWOOD relationship was with *Jimmy Kimmel Live!* The exposure
would hugely benefit our School SCRABBLE Program and the National School SCRABBLE Championship. The
catalyst in all this was Jimmy's brilliant producer Jill Leiderman.
She had left a similar position at *Late Night with David Letterman*
to take over Jimmy's show when it was still struggling in ratings
after the launch.

Through talent, perseverance, and patience, Jimmy and Jill
went on to build the show into the highly successful entity it is
today. So we were understandably thrilled when it was proposed
in 2007 that Jimmy challenge the newly crowned National School
SCRABBLE champions to a SCRABBLE match on the show.

As it turned out, that championship team, Aune Mitchell and
Matthew Silver, was historical. She was the only female ever to
play on a winning NSSC team, and Matthew was the first to win
two NSSCs—each with a different partner.

Jimmy Kimmel is a serious SCRABBLE player. That had been made apparent to me previously in LA at a St. Jude's Children's Hospital celebrity SCRABBLE tournament, where he was the winner and damn proud of it. So I knew he had no intention of taking it easy on the kids. Plus, the kids would be in for some good-natured trash-talking from Jimmy, as that's what the show is all about. No problem.

However, we did have one concern. Jimmy and the kids would be playing a "lightning round" version of SCRABBLE: the first side to reach 150 points would win. While I had little doubt the kids were much better players—sorry, Jimmy—this format would overemphasize the luck factor should someone get great tiles early.

And that's exactly what happened. Jimmy and his partner, Joe Rogan of *Fear Factor* fame, got the tiles to play the word SPAC-ERS for 76 points for an early, ultimately insurmountable, lead. Graciously, Jimmy acknowledged this.

To the show's credit, the format was changed going forward to reduce the luck factor, and the contests immediately became closer. There were other changes as well. One was the over-sized, customized SCRABBLE board the show's prop depart-ment designed and built for play. I've seen scores of custom-made boards over the years, and this was one of the most impressive in regard to both size and craftsmanship.

Another change was adding me to the segment as the offi-cial judge and word authority in case there were any challenges. While I'd been on television many times, I knew this would be more demanding for a couple of reasons. First, I would be responsible for verifying the score after each turn, which could be a heady prospect in a fast-paced game in front of a live studio audience. Second, I would be another person onstage to be a target for Jimmy's barbs. In other words, there was the potential for me to look stupid in any number of ways!

I didn't disappoint. It turned out that my vantage point to see the plays—behind an elevated podium a few feet away—was less than perfect. I also couldn't calculate the score quickly, or always accurately, because all the bonus squares were covered immediately by the play. So I was struggling to remember where, say, the double-letter square was while doing math in my head at the same time. On national television.

This scenario was compounded by the fact that the players knew their scores—and announced them aloud—the moment they made the play. So I was playing catch-up, which made for awkward dead-air time. At one point, as I struggled to verify the play, Jimmy looked over to me and said, "John, you're pretty much useless up here, aren't you?" The audience howled.

▪ ▪ ▪

Our trips to LA and the *Kimmel* show were always highlighted by the time the kid champs and I spent hanging out poolside at the Hollywood Roosevelt Hotel, surely one of the most surreal and decadent spots in the country.

The pool area at the Hollywood Roosevelt is right out of a movie—literally. You've seen it dozens of times on television shows such as *Entourage* and in numerous films. The hotel is usually utilized to make a statement about, or at least establish an atmosphere of, Hollywood hedonism. There are dozens of beautiful young women in scant swimsuits and an equal number of toned young men. There are also the obligatory band members and their groupies. The musicians are invariably the pale, gaunt, bearded guys off in the corner—working-class English accents optional.

Two demographics not represented at the Hollywood Roosevelt pool scene are preteen SCRABBLE experts and sixty-year-old white guys. In other words, us. So one of my favorite things to do every year was to head down to the pool with the kids and set up a game of SCRABBLE right in the middle of all this. I should add the pool is packed pretty much every day, all day long. I'm not sure what all these people do for work. In fact, hardly anyone even swims. They are there to be seen.

With the exception of that first year, the team of young SCRABBLE champions was always boys, around twelve or thirteen years old. It goes without saying that none of them have ever seen anything quite like this scene. While I hoped the distraction of all these young women would give me an advantage in our poolside match, it rarely happened. It takes more than a string bikini or wet T-shirt to break the focus of these young word wizards.

Invariably people would drift over, mostly wondering who we were and why the hell we are there. As soon as they spotted the SCRABBLE board, the questions and comments started.

"Oh, SCRABBLE, I used to play with my grandmother. Then she died, so we stopped playing."

"Is this like Words with Friends?"

"Are these kids, like, good at this?"

"I see a word!"

When I told them who the kids were and that we were going to appear on *Jimmy Kimmel Live!*, their interest went up a few degrees. Among the comments after this revelation:

"Do you know Jimmy?"

"Can I get tickets?"

"Who else is on the show tonight?"

"My cousin is in a band. Can you give Jimmy their CD for me?"

■ ■ ■

Rehearsals were always fun. The kids and their parents would go over to the studio for a tour, and then we'd sit down and work out the segment. Jimmy wasn't around for this, of course, but his producer Josh Weintraub stood in for him as we rehearsed. Josh is damn funny in his own right and put the kids—and their parents—at ease.

The entire staff at the *Kimmel* show was the best I ever worked with in twenty-five years of doing both media appearances and television production. Their attention to detail, their consideration, their attitude, and their professionalism were exceptional, from the security guard at the door to Jimmy himself. They had two goals: make it a great experience for the kids and make good television. Oh yeah, having Jimmy emerge victorious might be a third priority.

Josh would tell the kids up front that Jimmy was going to tease them and give them a lot of good-natured ribbing. After the first year or two, the kids pretty much knew this from seeing previous shows, and they were cool with it.

Josh actually encouraged the kids to give it back to Jimmy, and sometimes they did. One year, Jimmy asked two-time winners Andy Hoang and Erik Salgado if their victory had been a big news story in their home state of North Carolina. "Yeah," Andy piped up, "we were right there on the front page of the newspaper along with war, death, and all that stuff." Both the audience and Jimmy cracked up.

Perhaps the most dramatic exchanges came from the 2010 champ, Bradley Robbins from New Hampshire. Bradley was one of the better young NSSC players of all time. He was also painfully shy, quiet, and not especially animated. But we all witnessed a metamorphosis of Jekyll-and-Hyde proportions when it was show time.

I'm not sure whether it was Josh Weintraub's enthusiastic coaching, but it was a very different young Bradley Robbins who sat across the SCRABBLE board from Jimmy Kimmel that night. Bradley fired back at every quip Jimmy made with a pretty good comeback of his own. His partner, Evan McCarthy, almost did a double take on the third exchange. I can't remember exactly what it was, but basically Jimmy had made a scoring mistake and Bradley suggested the talk show host brush up on his basic math in addition to his spelling skills. It was spontaneous and fun to watch.

Some people in the SCRABBLE community thought Bradley had crossed the line in being too sassy. But he was only doing what he'd been coached to do. He'd also reached deep into himself and found something neither he nor us knew was there. Jimmy took it all in stride. However, I did have one parent of a potential School Champion express reluctance to have her child on the show. "I don't want him to do what Bradley Robbins was encouraged to do," she told me.

Several years later, Bradley Robbins plays tournament SCRABBLE on the adult circuit, but he's moved on to other things as well. He goes by the name of Brad and is an aspiring rapper.

As I write this, I know my career as a *Jimmy Kimmel Live!*

guest is over. But I'll be forever thankful to Jimmy and the show for giving us a chance to showcase both our national School SCRABBLE Program and the remarkable student champions.

▪ ▪ ▪

All this reminds me of my one television appearance that did not happen. That would be in 2004 when I was asked about being on *The Daily Show with Jon Stewart.* The circumstances were less than ideal. It was the offensive-words topic all over again.

It began at the 2004 National SCRABBLE Championship in New Orleans. It was, in fact, the only time we ever had an NSC on ESPN. During our preproduction meetings the issue of having potentially offensive words on television came up. After discussions, it was agreed with veteran ESPN producer David Stern that we would handle it in the following manner: during the twenty-eight games leading up to the televised finals, the players could play any words they wanted, but for the finals, ESPN—and the NSA—would have to impose a ban on certain words.

These were the same words disallowed for the kids' championship, most of which coincided with a list of words the network had banned on its own. Predictably, most everyone thought this was absurd, but that was the reality if we were going to have SCRABBLE on television.

Of particular interest and amusement was the word RED-SKINS. An ethnic slur, it had been a no-no on the SCRABBLE offensive-words list since day one. But ESPN used the word routinely when reporting about the pro football team of the same name. So the dilemma arose as to the acceptability of REDSKINS for the telecast. As the old saying goes, you can't make this stuff up. As I write this, ten years later, the Washington team is under increased pressure to change its name. Most feel it's only a matter of time.

So we get to the finals of Trey Wright versus David Gibson, both great guys and friends of mine. At one point in the game, Trey laid down the word LEZ. Both players nodded and wrote the score down, and Trey fished in the bag for three new tiles. Only then did we all realize the word could not be played on television. Chaos ensued in both the viewing room and the production booth.

We had to stop play immediately. Then we had to explain to both players and the crowd of three hundred spectators in an adjoining screening room what had happened. No one was happy. Trey was understandably upset. Gibson, being Gibson, was totally sympathetic. And the audience, most of whom were tournament SCRABBLE players, was jeering.

Worse, I had no idea what to do. Time stood still as I tried to figure out a solution. This exact situation had never happened in the twenty-five-plus years of tournament SCRABBLE, so I had no precedent for reference. Meanwhile, the players were twitching, the audience was squirming, and the cameras were idle. The one thing I *did* know was that I was not going to make this ruling by myself.

I announced that we were going to take a break. I then asked all the members of the NSA Advisory Board to gather for an emergency meeting. Once assembled, we reviewed all the various options we had. Ultimately, it was decided that Trey would withdraw the play without penalty, put his new tiles back in the bag, and make another play. Graciously, Trey did as we asked. He made a lesser play but still won the game and the championship.

However, that was far from the end of it. Among the spectators who witnessed this debacle was SCRABBLE tournament player Whitney Gould. I knew Whitney, and knew her to be a smart and very cool person. She's also a journalist. And she's based in San Francisco. As you might imagine, the LEZ controversy would be of interest to any reporter, especially one from a San Francisco newspaper.

So as this was all happening, Whitney approached me and said she was going to file a story with, I believe, the *San Francisco Chronicle*. She was almost apologetic, but I told her that as a writer myself I completely understood.

Over the years there have been basically two flash points where I knew the media would be all over us: the offensive words and cheating. Try as we might to generate stories about SCRABBLE's legacy, educational benefits, interesting people, big-money tournaments, and the rest, nothing appealed to the media as much as the sensationalism of dirty words and dirty play. In other words, Whitney's story went viral.

This led to the usual and demanding routine of explaining what happened, our position, and all the rest. As was always the case, I got to be the point man in the debacle.

At the height of all this, I received a call from a producer at *The Daily Show* who said the LEZ story had caught their eye. The show was looking for someone to come on to "explain" what had happened. That would be me. A fan of the show, I was at first excited about the prospect. Then I realized that "explain what happened" actually meant "defend your ridiculous position."

I'd failed to consider one fatal flaw. I could be as funny and articulate as I wanted, but it's the job of *The Daily Show* to make me look foolish, stupid, or both. At the end of the day, I'd be no different to them from an arrogant NRA spokesman, Tea Party zealot, or corporate shill. And as soon as I was off camera, they could use charts, graphs, stock footage, commentary, and Jon Stewart himself to make me look like a clown. Sadly, that probably happens enough on its own; I don't have to go looking for it.

I declined the appearance.

14

WORDPLAY

ANY SERIOUS SCRABBLE COMPETITOR CAN TELL you two things in a nanosecond: his or her best play of all time and the anagram of his or her name. It comes with the turf. My best play was CONQUEST for 221 points. It was a "triple-triple" extending from one triple word square to the next for nine times the value, plus a 50-point bonus for using all my tiles. The Q was already on the board.

If you are lucky enough to have a nice blend of vowels and consonants in your name, chances are as many as a half-dozen curious and fun phrases can be made from the letters. When I first started being serious about SCRABBLE years ago, all of us had to painstakingly shuffle the letters on our rack to try to find the words within. As with so many other things, technology has now made it possible to achieve in forty-five seconds what used to take forty-five minutes. Just Google the word ANAGRAM and you'll find numerous sites that will anagram any word or phrase, including your name. Don't forget to use your middle or maiden name for variety or flexibility.

The first time my name was anagrammed was by my NSA colleague Joe Edley. We worked with John Dunbar Williams, leaving out the JR or JUNIOR. The first one Joe configured was ADMAN JOB WILL RUSH IN. This one was particularly apt, as before I started my SCRABBLE career, I was a partner and creative director of a small advertising agency. That said, anagrams of people's names are even more fun to me when they are beyond random with no context whatsoever. For example, the second anagram Edley came up with for my name was I HURL WILDMAN'S BANJO. Huh?

Joe Edley loves to anagram. He's convinced that, designed and marketed properly, an anagramming-based game could someday become as popular as SCRABBLE, Monopoly, or Trivial Pursuit. Call me skeptical—or even cynical—but I just don't see that happening in an increasingly dumbed-down America. Well, maybe if the anagrams were limited to three or four letters.

My family and I were once having dinner with Joe near Philadelphia after a SCRABBLE tournament at, of all places, the Franklin Mint. (The Mint had just launched a super-duper SCRABBLE set with 24K gold-plated tiles, and the tournament was a promotional event we set up with them.) After we had finished our meal, the waitress approached the table and asked if we'd like to hear about the desserts. We agreed.

"Well," she began, "tonight our specialty is peach melba."

Without missing a beat, Edley shouted out, "Cheap Blame!"—an anagram for the dessert name.

As the waitress stood there stunned and confused, my teenage daughter and her friend dove under the table in embarrassment. Grinning, my wife faked a cough into her napkin while I tried to explain, which was almost more embarrassing.

This kind of thing happens all the time when you hang out with SCRABBLE players. During the 1998 National Championship in Chicago, one of our event interns, Ben Lyons, who went on to become an entertainment reporter and ESPN radio host, decided to attend a Cubs game with a group of tournament competitors. I asked him later how the game was; he shrugged and said it was okay. When pressed, he said it was tough to watch because some of his companions seemed more excited about anagramming the names on the back of the players' jerseys than about the action in the game.

As a matter of fact, baseball is the overwhelming favorite among sports for the SCRABBLE crowd. For openers, it is very strategic, and the pace is decidedly slow. (A major-league baseball game lasts, on average, three hours. The average SCRABBLE tournament game is forty-five to fifty minutes. The average living room game can last twice as long, depending on the number of players and disagreements.) Then there's the massive amount of statistics and mountains of esoteric knowledge to discover, memorize, and have ready should you ever need it. Just like obscure words. Most sports fans agree that baseball is the "geeks' sport." Not only do you have all that crazy stuff to know, it's only marginally athletic. Don't get me wrong. I love baseball, but it is the only sport where at any given time, sixteen of the eighteen participants are either standing still or sitting down. After the recently formed NASPA—more on that later—the two organizations most tournament players belong to are probably Mensa and SABR, the six-thousand-member Society for American Baseball Research.

The latter is a group devoted to the compilation and analysis of baseball statistics. At their annual conventions, new evidence might be presented that could change a long-held record. For example, someone might have uncovered an obscure newspaper article or letter that casts doubt on a home run hit by Babe Ruth in 1931—thus changing his lifetime total from 714 home runs to a mere 713. While insignificant to most Americans, this is as exciting to this group as the admission of QI to North American SCRABBLE was to me. I get it. (Note: my example of Babe Ruth's bogus home run was purely hypothetical. Please, no calls or letters!)

■ ■ ■

A wonderful anagram moment took place in Los Angeles during the 1994 National SCRABBLE Championship. I was having dinner with a group that included World SCRABBLE Champion Mark Nyman, who's English, and veteran American expert Robert Kahn. After dinner the group stood outside the restaurant and chatted. I happened to look across the street and spot a large red neon sign that said SHERATON.

I studied the letters, convinced there must have been—given the favorable letters—several good anagrams. Yet after a few minutes I'd come up empty. Frustrated, I tapped Nyman and pointed to the sign.

"Mark, there's got to be a couple of good anagrams in there, right?"

Nyman stared at it for no more than two seconds. "No, sorry. But with an I, you'd have ANTIHEROS." The word is acceptable in the Collins international SCRABBLE dictionary but not in North America—although ANTIHEROES is.

I remember thinking that I could study anagramming flash cards ten hours a day for the rest of my life and I could never do that. Later, I wished I'd asked Robert Kahn, a superb anagrammer, the same question. Robert once played the word UNREALIZED from a SCRABBLE rack of AEILNRU, adding it to the ZED that was already on the board. He also once scored 801 points in a match, the second-highest total in history. The record is 830 by Michael Cresta in an official Boston club game in Lexington, Massachusetts, on October 12, 2006.

Probably the funniest anagram story was told to me by the writer and talk show host Dick Cavett a number of years ago. We were both presenters at the annual Wonderful World of Words Weekend at the Mohonk Mountain House resort in New Paltz, New York. The event was created by word lover and game expert Gloria Rosenthal and her husband, Larry, and now run by Will Shortz. If you're reading this book and finding it at all engaging, then you owe yourself a visit to this amazing venue. It's a weekend packed with mind-boggling puzzles, serious game playing, and programs and lectures by people like Ira Glass, Cavett, and Stephen Sondheim. I've been honored to present twice.

Anyway, Cavett and I got to talking anagrams. He told me that he was essentially an "anagramming savant" and that anagrams just popped into his head on a regular and random basis. Cavett's best story concerned an appearance on Johnny Carson's *Tonight Show*. During Dick's conversation with Johnny they were talking about—among other things—former vice president Spiro Agnew. The conversation went on to other topics; then other guests came on, and Dick moved down the guest couch.

As Cavett told it, later in the show Carson was interviewing an actress about her new movie when Cavett suddenly and loudly blurted out, "Grow a penis!" The conversation screeched to a halt. The entire studio went silent as a thousand eyes bored in on Cavett. Flustered, he hurriedly went into an explanation about how Spiro Agnew's name anagrammed into GROW A PENIS. Laughter ensued. This anecdote is now part of the Anagramming Awards Hall of Fame at Anagrammy.com.

Obviously, anagrams are a critical part of the SCRABBLE skill set. If you've got AEIMNRS on your rack, you'd better be able to find MARINES, REMAINS, or SEMINAR or you're in for a long game. It's important to know that these skills can absolutely be developed and improved. There are numerous Internet study aids for practice. Those most favored by tournament players include Zyzzyva, Quackle, and Zarf.

The typical exercise below is at a level for most good casual players. Find an anagram for the each word. Answers are in the appendix.

1. PYRIC
2. CHURL
3. TRADED
4. SADDLE
5. RACOON
6. NASTILY
7. PAYOUTS
8. BEEFIER
9. DROOLED
10. EXCLAIMS
11. SPAWNING
12. INDULGED

No discourse on anagrams would be complete without examples of some of the better ones floating out there in the world of word lovers:

DORMITORY	Dirty room
EVANGELIST	Evil's agent
DESPERATION	A rope ends it
THE MORSE CODE	Here come the dots
MOTHER-IN-LAW	Woman Hitler
SNOOZE ALARMS	Alas! No more Z's
ELEVEN PLUS TWO	Twelve plus one
CLINT EASTWOOD	Old West action
SLOT MACHINES	Cash lost in 'em
CONVERSATION	Voices rant on
NORWEGIANS	Swen or Inga?
THE PIANO BENCH	Beneath Chopin
SOUTHERN CALIFORNIA	Hot sun or life in a car

PALINDROMES

And, of course, no conversation about anagrams would be complete without at least mentioning their complicated, confounding cousin—palindromes. A palindrome is a phrase, name or sentence that reads the same backward and forward. Common examples include:

STEP ON NO PETS

A MAN, A PLAN, A CANAL: PANAMA

If anagrams have at least one useful purpose—improving your SCRABBLE game—palindromes' one purpose is mind-boggling amusement. I'd never even think of attempting to create a palindrome, let along completing one!

One of the more interesting people in the word world is a fellow named Jon Agee. A gifted illustrator and gamer, Jon is considered one of the country's foremost palindromists as well. He is the author of such books as *ELVIS LIVES! and Other Anagrams; SIT ON A POTATO PAN, OTIS! More Palindromes*; and *PALINDROMANIA!* Jon is one of the most creative and original people I've ever met.

Astoundingly, Jon once told me that he could not really understand anagrams and why anyone would do them. This coming from a guy who does *palindromes!* Jon and I were doing a mutual book signing many years ago when a woman asked him to inscribe her copy.

"To whom shall I sign it?" Jon asked.

The woman replied, "Naomi."

"I moan!" Jon blurted out immediately.

Here's another fun story involving Jon Agee. Many years ago, a bunch of us had assembled at the home of Gloria and Larry Rosenthal, the Wonderful World of Words creators, for one of their periodic, heavy-duty game-play sessions. Gloria is a writer and former word-game editor for *Games* magazine and Larry a retired veteran of Madison Avenue.

An evening at the Rosenthals' always featured serious, high-level gamers who got together to play obscure, intense games and often test out new games from inventors. Guests that night included Will Shortz, Jon, David Feldman, a tournament bridge player, author, and game master, and me. I should add that, while respectable at most games, I was in way over my head in this crowd.

After a couple of hours of games, we decided to head down to a local restaurant for dinner. It was a beautiful summer evening, and I wanted to show off my new convertible. So Jon and Will jumped in with me, while David Feldman went with the Rosenthals.

About halfway to the restaurant, we stopped at a red light. Almost immediately, a car with three women in it pulled up next to us. All of us were in our thirties and forties and, I'd like to think, checked each other out for perhaps a second or two. Then the light changed and everyone zoomed off. I remember thinking later: Man, if those women only knew! Those three guys in the convertible? The crossword editor of the *New York Times*, the country's foremost palindromist, and the executive director of the National SCRABBLE Association! Talk about chick magnets!

15

ARE MEN REALLY BETTER
THAN WOMEN?

THE CONCEPT OF ONE GENDER BEING superior to the other at
SCRABBLE has been—with the possible exception of
the offensive-words controversy—the most discussed
and volatile topic among players for years. At face value, it seems
groundless, sexist, mean-spirited, and irrelevant. Yet it remains
a topic that just won't go away. Having participated in hundreds
of interviews over my years on the job, I'd have to say this is one
of the questions most often thrown at me by the press.

Let's start with some assumptions. First, it's widely accepted
by both academics and social scientists that women test better
than men in regard to language skills. So, theoretically, women
should be better at SCRABBLE, right? Wrong. Or at least not
necessarily.

As author Stefan Fatsis so beautifully nailed it in *Word Freak*,
SCRABBLE's "dirty little secret" is that it is about math. Also
widely accepted is that men test better at math than women.
At the very top level of the game, for example, it's pretty much

assumed that most of the top fifty or so players have committed all or most of the *Official SCRABBLE Players Dictionary* to memory. So that covers the word and language part of one's arsenal. That leaves the math-based skill set to determine superiority, which means having the ability to assess probability of tile possibilities. For example, there are twelve E's in the game; if seven have been played and there are only twenty-two tiles left, what are the odds your opponent has a vital E, or even two of them?

Another component in this skill set is what we call "board vision," the ability to look for—and find—every possibility on the board given your rack and position in the game. At the same time, you're performing multiple calculations and assessing spatial relationships. Of course, the deeper you are in the match, the more tiles have been played, so the more complicated the calculations are—and you're performing them for both yourself on offense and for your opponent as part of your defense.

On the day I wrote this, I went to the marvelous website Cross-tables.com. Created by players Keith Smith and Seth Lipkin, it is by far the most comprehensive collection of data from decades of official SCRABBLE tournaments. It features player rankings, ratings, tournament results, best plays, standings, highlights, and pretty much any other data one might want to know about themselves and other tournament players. (*Please bear in mind that the ratings and rankings discussed here were researched well before the publication date and certainly have changed, but the analysis is still valid.*)

I decided to review the statistics on Cross-tables.com to check the number of women listed in the Top 25 players in North America. There was one: Canadian Robin Pollock Daniel in twenty-fifth place. Maybe more disheartening for women is that a thirteen-year-old boy, Mack Meller of New York, was ranked eighth. Granted, Mack is the current prodigy in a game culture that has only seen a handful in forty years, but still. What's the deal?

If we look deeper down the list, through the Top 50, we find two more women. Expand it to the Top 100 and the number of females rises to seven. Equally as inexplicable is the fact that only one woman has won a National SCRABBLE Championship in the history of the event. That was Rita Norr in 1987.

An unassuming role model, Rita, who died in 2010 at just sixty-six years old, was smart and gracious. She told me a number of times that she felt extremely fortunate to have won and was mystified why twenty-five years later her accomplishment was never duplicated.

So let's agree that, despite disturbing conclusions, we'll throw out the statistical evidence regarding male supremacy across the SCRABBLE board. How else could one explain it?

One theory is that men as a group still have more of a cultural imperative to be competitive and dominant, whether the venue is business, sports, board games, charades, whatever. Personally, I believe this will change over time as a couple of generations of young girls compete equally with and against boys in soccer, Little League baseball, and the like.

Perhaps the best theory was put forth by veteran *Sports Illustrated* writer S. L. (Scott) Price, who wrote a brilliant piece on tournament SCRABBLE back in 1995. After Scott spent some time with top-level tournament SCRABBLE players, he issued this simple explanation. "Forget about all your fancy theories," he told me. "Men are better at SCRABBLE than women because . . . *women aren't that nuts!*"

Men do have an affinity for trivia, collecting, and focusing on one thing to the exclusion of others. In my experience, women, not so much. Scott and I talked about how it's boys and men who early on memorize baseball statistics, car features, and other arguably useless facts. It's an easy transition from that dubious pastime to studying and learning thousands of esoteric words that no one else knows or uses. A cynical friend once suggested that a guy's knowledge of sports trivia is in indirect proportion to his actual athletic ability. More than one high school basketball team statistician has said to the team captain, "Sure, you can dunk a basketball. But do you know the name of Ty Cobb's parakeet?"

■　■　■

I decided to go right to the source and talk to three top female SCRABBLE players about their thoughts on the issue. The first was Robin Pollock Daniel, universally recognized for years as the top woman player in North America. While this is an enviable distinction, it's as if Robin walks around with an asterisk tattooed on her forehead. Why not just refer to her as one of the best players in the world?

Robin is distinctive for a number of reasons. She's scary smart, she's funny, and she's generous of spirit. The mother of two boys, Robin has worked professionally as a copywriter, a researcher, and a psychologist, among other things. While she is feared and respected by top players internationally, a major championship win has eluded her.

It certainly isn't for the lack of trying. Robin is one of the most dedicated students of the game ever. She spends three or four hours a day whenever possible studying words, playing online, or conducting tireless replays of previous matches—both hers and others. There's a word-study program at Zyzzyva.net created by the brilliant Michael Thelen, where players can second-guess their peers' moves and analyze "best play" in various situations. The artificial intelligence will tell them how often they find the best play, the second-best play, and so on. Robin routinely finds the best play 90 percent of the time!

Even when she first started out as a tournament player almost thirty years ago, it was clear where Robin was headed. She won a Best Newcomer Award and in her second year of play jumped from a 1544 rating to a 1750 rating in one tournament! The Expert rating starts at 1600. Most people get there incrementally—often over a span of several years. Robin Pollock Daniel did it in one giant leap, and she never looked back.

Robin has been ranked as high as third overall—for both genders—and says the overriding thing to remember is that "tournament SCRABBLE is a meritocracy at the end of the day. It's really that simple." As a result, she says, men always accept her as an equal. Her record speaks for itself. "If anyone felt I was a bit fraudulent playing among the big boys, it was me—not them," she adds.

I asked her about being referred to as "the best *woman* SCRABBLE player in the world." Robin chooses not to see it as dismissive or qualifying. "It doesn't bother me in the least," she asserts. "I like it because at the end of the day I think of myself as a teacher, a mentor. It gives me credibility that I can leverage to help other women." When I kidded Robin about her fierce, word-nerdish study habits, more associated with men than with women, she laughed. "Yeah, well, as Woody Allen says, men cite statistics to delay orgasm."

Like the other women experts I interviewed, Robin is not hopeful that the situation will improve anytime soon for women tournament players. For whatever reason—biological, cultural, etc.—the statistics say it all. "It's the same now as it's always been," Robin laments. Despite the changes in the last twenty years—the introduction of the National School SCRABBLE Program, more tournaments, Internet play, new study techniques, and more—the rankings tell the same story. "We're very lucky if there are three women in the Top 50 at any given time."

A quick look at the results of the National School SCRABBLE Championship bears this out. That event is now over a dozen years old. Competitors are grouped in teams of two, which means there have been forty-eight finalists in all those years. Only one has been female: Aune Mitchell, daughter of well-known SCRABBLE organizer and coach Cornelia Guest. Aune was on the winning team in 2007 with Matthew Silver; she no longer competes regularly in tournaments.

Out of curiosity, I decided to check out the male/female ratio for the National Spelling Bee. More established and better known than the National School SCRABBLE Championship, the bee arguably targets the same type of kid and the same ages, fifth to eighth grade. In theory, School SCRABBLE, if properly managed, has the potential to overtake the spelling bee in the future. Let's face it, for most of us, SCRABBLE is a lot more fun than standing up in front of a bunch of people, trembling as you try to visualize, then correctly spell a twelve-letter word that even a World SCRABBLE Champion would not know. And when was the last time any of us participated in a spelling bee? A person can play SCRABBLE for his or her entire life.

In reviewing the results of the National Spelling Bee over

the last dozen years, we find that girls have won forty-six times through 2013. While not dominant, it is certainly statistically superior to their performance at SCRABBLE and better than boys, who've won the National Spelling Bee forty-one times.

Now let's look at crossword puzzle competition. Will Shortz, organizer of the annual American Crossword Puzzle Tournament, confirms that women have won that event three times in thirty-six years and finished second a dozen times. Will attributes women's better showing at crossword puzzles to the following reason: "SCRABBLE is almost purely a math game at its essence, which favors males, whereas crosswords blend some math acuity along with word skills and knowledge of various facts."

▪   ▪   ▪

I next posed the gender question to Lisa Odom of St. Louis Park, Minnesota, another perennial top female competitor. Lisa started playing tournaments in 1989, having become hooked on the game in what was at the time the semiunderground New York club scene. This was the SCRABBLE world before *Word Freak* or SCRABBLE on ESPN. A time when tournament players still toiled in obscurity and sometimes only as few as a dozen players would show up at a handful of locations – a friendly restaurant, a church basement, or a YMCA. Everyone pretty much knew everyone else, and strangers entered at their own risk. Newbies and curious living room players were often treated with a blend of bemusement and contempt, and only the hard core would return.

Lisa Odom not only joined this scene, she thrived. Lisa's credentials are impressive. She has been the only female member of the American team in the World SCRABBLE Championship three times, in 1993, 1999, and 2005. She was also one of a handful of women who competed in the $100,000 SCRABBLE Superstars Showdown in Las Vegas in 1995. In addition, Lisa is one of the few women in history to be a member of the 2000 Club, the most elite rating designation among tournament players—those who have been rated over 2000 in the official rankings. As of June 2014, only thirteen tournament players were rated 2000 or above. In addition, Lisa has also been ranked as high as sixth overall among the thousands of players who maintain ratings.

When asked to rate her competitive nature on a scale of 1 to 10, Lisa hesitated, then replied, laughing, "If I'm honest, probably an 8 or 9. But I wasn't always that way. It evolved over time." It must make for interesting games at home, as Lisa's husband, Steve Pellinen, is also a veteran top SCRABBLE expert and tournament organizer.

Lisa's approach to competition and SCRABBLE has evolved as well. During our conversation, she shared a personal mantra she has developed. It is the acronym LOVE: Look, Overlook, Verify, Evaluate.

Look simply means look over the complete board for all opportunities for both yourself and your opponent. *Overlook* means repeat that exact same exercise. It's amazing how many times players are certain they've found the best play—only to find a better one after one more pass over the board. *Verify* means make sure the play is good, the word acceptable. *Evaluate* means carefully assess that the play you are about to make is the best move. This, of course, means the best *strategic* move, not necessarily the most points. They are not always the same. Just ask anyone who's played some of the weaker SCRABBLE apps out there. For them, it's always about points only! Why? Because very often no SCRABBLE experts were consulted when the manufacturers and marketers designed these apps.

As we discussed, a good SCRABBLE move is comprised of what you put on the board to score with and what you leave on your rack to work with. For example, let's say you score 37 points but leave yourself the tiles U, U, V, C. Sure, you scored some points, but you are going to have terrible racks for the next several turns because of your terrible tile "leave." A better play—strategically—would be to play off a couple of those tough tiles or exchange them for new ones.

Predictably, Lisa is a keen student of the game. She studies about five hours a week, she says, and once recorded and analyzed every game she played for an entire year using Quackle, the genius SCRABBLE analysis software developed by Jason Katz-Brown while he was still an undergraduate at MIT. "I took a year off between jobs," explains Lisa, who works in health care, "and, believe me, nothing helps your SCRABBLE career more than being unemployed!"

Like her peers, Lisa is at a loss to explain the lack of female presence among the SCRABBLE competitive elite. "This is not rocket science," she insists. "Women should definitely be able to do this." That said, she agrees that the immediate future does not look good and that women have not yet caught up with men in SCRABBLE competitiveness. "I really hope one of us wins a World or National Championship again in my lifetime," Lisa said.

That led to a brief story about Rita Norr, a friend and mentor to Lisa. Rita was known for her sweetness but could also be tough. Lisa described a situation decades ago when Rita had researched and compiled a "3 to make 8 letters" word list on her own. Examples might be adding SEA to QUAKE to make SEAQUAKE or COT to QUEAN to make COTQUEAN. I know, I know. You're asking yourself, "Who would know this stuff?" I was flattered that Lisa assumed that I did.

Lisa kept asking Rita to share this secret list, but her friend refused for years. Remember, this was before computer-generated word lists existed. Many expert players hoarded their lists, not only for a competitive edge but because each represented perhaps a hundred hours of thankless, tedious research. In the end, though, Lisa's persistence and Rita's good nature prevailed and the list was shared.

As we ended our conversation, I asked Lisa to randomly tell me one of her favorite plays. She barely hesitated. "It was the word GOLGOTHA, played through an existing H on the board." It means "a burial ground." Like many people, I've seen the word over the years—but never on a SCRABBLE board!

■ ■ ■

Debbie Stegman is the sassy, smart girl you knew in high school. She has an MBA from Columbia University and spent nearly two decades pushing the proverbial glass ceiling to become a vice president of Warner Bros. In 2013, she decided to take a break from the corporate world to spend more time "being happy" and, of course, playing more SCRABBLE. Debbie is newer to the scene than both Lisa and Robin but no less tenacious with the tiles. She played in her first tournament in 2000 and has been on a fierce streak ever since. After just her second tournament, she was approached by a couple of top female experts who'd been watching the newcomer. "Some day, you are going to be one of us," they told her. That was all the motivation she needed.

The day we spoke, Debbie was ranked second among U.S. women and fifty-first overall. Debbie has a number of observations about the gender gap in tournament performance. She agrees with the other women I talked to that it all comes down to one's sense of competition. "I think women are more competitive within themselves as individuals, but not with other women," she suggests.

Debbie also says she's noticed an interesting gender-based dynamic at tournaments. "When a guy breaks away from the pack to take a decent lead in the field, everyone silently roots against him. Not on a personal level—at least most of the time— but because if he falters, their own chances improve. It's logical and natural." But on the rare occasion when a woman breaks away from the pack, she can almost feel all the other females bonding in support. "Women don't root against each other," Debbie says.

Like Lisa and Robin, Debbie does not feel as if her male opponents are ever holding back or deferring to her in any way. She's just another expert. I ask her if she ever feels it's an advantage being a woman in a division full of men. She pauses. "Not really," she muses, "although I'm not above putting on some fresh lipstick if I think it might distract my opponent."

Asked for one of her memorable plays, Debbie goes back to a match at the notoriously tough Manhattan SCRABBLE Club in midtown. One night, in a casual team game, Debbie was partnered with champions Robert Felt and Joel Sherman. In this situation, it's understood in the SCRABBLE culture that the lesser player pretty much sits in silence—just observe and learn.

But at one point in the game, Debbie just couldn't help her-self. As Felt and Sherman intensely studied their rack and the board for the best play, Debbie impulsively grabbed the tiles and, in one swift move, laid down the word SCIENTISTS.

The table was stunned. The weakest player—a woman no less—had thrown down a *ten-letter word*! Even more astonishing is that the play was through disconnected letters already on the board. In other words, it's not as if TIS was there and Debbie simply built around it. No, she wove her way through. This is classic board vision, and it doesn't get any better than that.

When I ask Debbie about the future fate of female players, she says she is not encouraged by what she sees: "It doesn't look good for us." She notes that while participation in the National School SCRABBLE Program is roughly even gender-wise, for the most part only the boys seem to go on past the eighth grade and enter the world of adult play. The same with prodigies. There has never been a female SCRABBLE prodigy of the caliber of Brian Cap-pelletto, Adam Logan, or the current young star Mack Meller.

As the father of two daughters, and as a male who grew up in a house filled with sisters, a mother, and a live-in aunt, I remain as discouraged as Robin, Lisa, and Debbie for the prospect of another female World or National SCRABBLE Champion. In fact, it appears the odds are much better that we'll have a female president first. And I'm okay with that.

16

THE END GAME

FEW MAJOR THINGS IN LIFE END when or how we presume they will. That marriage was over long before that first, raw, stilted visit to the couples counselor. Your favorite team's championship hopes were exhausted long before they were mathematically eliminated. Sometimes the ending is a protracted, abstract, corrosive process that seemingly happened while you were asleep. Other times it can be an abrupt, unexpected bombshell, a veritable Dear John letter that arrives with a benumbing thud.

I knew my SCRABBLE career would end someday. I just didn't know when, how, or why.

I had specifically addressed "the end" a dozen years ago with Stefan Fatsis in *Word Freak*. Interviewed at the NSA's height of activity, I cautioned that it was unrealistic to assume this streak would last indefinitely. Over the course of my career, I'd worked for and with some fairly heady companies. They included not just Hasbro but Nickelodeon, Simon & Schuster, IBM, ESPN, MTV

Networks, Merriam-Webster, CNN, Paramount, and numerous others. I'd been around the block. I'd learned firsthand the truth of the old adage that the only thing in business that remains the same is change—so be ready for it.

Working with Hasbro—and previous SCRABBLE owners Selchow & Righter and Coleco—I'd probably collaborated with two hundred executives over the years. Some became friends and colleagues for decades. Others were simply bit players in the process. More than once, at all three companies that owned the game, my team and I had been told we would be working with a new executive who would be our point person for all SCRABBLE activities—only to find that person had been reassigned, had left, or had been fired before we'd even had a single meeting.

Navigating through the phalanx of executives was, of course, the most difficult part of the job. Nearly a dozen times, I had to journey up to Hasbro Games headquarters in East Longmeadow, Massachusetts, and tell the SCRABBLE story to a new corporate team or key executive who'd transferred from another part of the company—or who'd never been in the game industry until a few weeks beforehand. My task included explaining the evolution of the game and its marketing strategies, the tournament scene as a marketing and public relations tool, opportunities their predecessors had missed, potential pitfalls, and more.

I learned my ultimate approach to all this from an old friend and colleague, Fred Seibert, one of the smartest people I know. Among other things, Fred, along with partner Alan Goodman, was on the founding staff for MTV and an architect of both Nickelodeon and Spike TV. Fred went on to become president of Hanna-Barbera, president of MTV Online, an Emmy Award–winning producer, and all kinds of other stuff. Fred is always around the action. As I write this, he was just acknowledged in the *Los Angeles Times* as the primary guru to the young man who launched the Internet sensation Tumblr.

One day at lunch, Fred told me this: "I was free when I totally accepted that some people in business are going to see me as a genius and others were going to think I'm a complete jerk." The key, of course, is to keep the latter group to a minimum—and to be aware of who is in which camp.

The second part is tricky. For understandable reasons, people don't often show their hand in business dealings. Hey, we're humans. That means, depending on the scenario, we're going to be defensive, territorial, paranoid, ambitious, confident, vindictive, or any of a host of other mindsets. Being an experienced game player—whether it's SCRABBLE or poker—can be helpful in the business world. We learn to size up situations and other participants quickly. We learn to recognize "tells" from people across the table. We understand when to be aggressive and when to lay back. We think strategically.

In working with SCRABBLE executives over the years, I bore this in mind. I also employed several other approaches in my M.O. First, I tried to get to know everyone—and understand them—as well as I could, both as people and as business partners. I worked hard to cultivate relationships at all levels—assistants, middle management, senior management. I worked hard for inclusion, always leaving a paper trail whenever I could to both cover my ass and get everyone involved.

I tried never to go over anyone's head unless it was absolutely necessary. Even then, I'd try to make sure the aggrieved party knew it was happening. No one was ever sucker-punched. Still, I know I pissed off some people along the way. But I don't regret it. My motivation was never to flex my influence or steamroll my agenda. Instead, I clung to my mantra. At the end of the day, my decisions and actions were never about what was best for me, the game's manufacturers, or the thousands of hardcore enthusiasts. It was "Always what's best for SCRABBLE, the game."

When Stefan and I discussed my future and that of the NSA, I said that neither I nor the NSA members should ever take anything for granted. The routine changing of the corporate guard, the economy, and budgets made us all vulnerable to both whimsy and legitimate new marketing philosophies. It's well understood in the business world that when a new senior executive arrives, there's a coattail loaded with his or her people waiting for their chance. This can be former ad and PR agencies, former right-hand men and women, and relatives.

So I knew well that it might happen—no, *would* happen—at some point. It would be when the people who "got" me and my approach were outnumbered by those who did not.

After two decades, the process of serious change began around 2007. At the time, the Hasbro marketing team we worked with in East Longmeadow, Massachusetts, was a thoughtful group who understood games and game culture. In a series of meetings, we all agreed that it was time to reprioritize the NSA's efforts. The consensus was that the NSA's time and talents would be better spent identifying and recruiting new players and game purchasers and less time on the day-to-day administration of the SCRABBLE tournament scene.

To achieve these new priorities, the NSA would first turn over many of our responsibilities to the players themselves. This would include, but not be limited to, the sanctioning and organization of both local tournaments and the National SCRABBLE

Championship, the management of three hundred or so official SCRABBLE Clubs in North America, all rules activities, development of word lists and materials, and revisions of the *Official SCRABBLE Players Dictionary*. The new group would also be responsible for maintaining a list of tournament ratings for up to 10,000 past and present tournament players and for selecting the team to represent the United States and Canada at the World SCRABBLE Championships. All these had been responsibilities of the NSA for decades. But not for much longer.

I both accepted and understood Hasbro's thinking on this. It was hard to argue with the logic when viewed through the lens of a contemplative, experienced business executive. Which is not to say it wasn't personally disappointing. Remember, part of me was a passionate player as well, with a perhaps unrealistic perspective of the game as sacred, not to be messed with by bottom-line-driven game marketers who "didn't understand" its magic and power.

When asked the best way to go about this transition, we proposed the following to Hasbro.

- That we organize a two-day SCRABBLE summit at Hasbro Games headquarters in East Longmeadow.
- The NSA would compile a list of fifteen NSA players to form a Steering Committee for the transition of selected responsibilities and invite them to the summit. The group would be diverse. It would include players, activists, and organizers from all over North America. Some would be top SCRABBLE experts. Others would be successful businesspeople. Still others would be average tournament players. There would be attorneys,

computer experts, parents with children in the School SCRABBLE Program, and more.

■ At the summit, the NSA staff, Hasbro Games executives, and the fifteen players would address the change and work out the next steps.

Part of me felt like a guy who was planning his own funeral. One of my survival skills has always been seeing change—or trouble—a mile away. This dynamic was honed at home, where both my parents were alcoholics. I could tell by the way the car door slammed when my father got home from work what the next several hours were going to be like. It was also developed at an all-boys Catholic school, where I basically tried to stay under the radar of the embittered monks who taught us and the tough kids freshly arrived to the suburbs from Brooklyn, Queens, and the Bronx. I realize this sounds very Dickensian, but that was what it felt like to me.

We began with an invitation to selected players. It was purposely vague, saying only that Hasbro wanted their input for a discussion on the future of organized SCRABBLE. They were thrilled. We explained that there would be some social aspects with numerous meals, a tour of the factory where they could actually see SCRABBLE being made right before their eyes, a gift package, and the like. And, of course, Hasbro paid all travel and hotel expenses.

So we convened, about twenty people altogether. The NSA was represented by Jane Ratsey Williams, Joe Edley, Katie Schulz Hukill, Patricia Hocker, and me. Our other key staff member, Theresa Bubb, held down the fort at NSA headquarters.

We started things off with a great cocktail party and dinner and kept things light. Hasbro execs mingled amiably with the players. We NSA staffers enjoyed ourselves as well, but the evening was compromised because of the hidden agenda we harbored.

Our meeting began the next day with introductions and some generalized overviews. Hasbro and I took turns explaining the upcoming changes and, to a lesser degree, the rationale behind it all. The group listened patiently. No one was particularly demonstrative in his or her reactions. Later, I surmised it was for a couple of reasons. For openers, there was plenty of vagueness about the transition. However, I believe that one fact stood out from the rest of the presentation and was the focus of the players: *after thirty years, they were finally going to have their own, solely player-run SCRABBLE association.*

This was a huge deal for them, and I knew it. This had been a dream for many of them for decades. And, despite the advances of player involvement in running the association under my tenure, there was always the perception—and I suppose the reality, too— that their fate was always in the hands of the Hasbro-supported NSA and the corporation itself.

This collective sentiment was made extremely clear as we opened the floor for discussion. I began with a proposal that we consider restructuring the NSA into two divisions. The first would be the Club and Tournament Division; this would be run completely by the players, with its own agenda and officers. The second would be the School SCRABBLE and Outreach Division. This would be run by the existing NSA staff. The two divisions would operate under the NSA umbrella.

It seemed like a reasonable and practical first step from my point of view. It would make the transition smoother; the new players group could benefit from our experience and relationship with Hasbro, and over time they could evolve to complete autonomy.

When I finished presenting this proposal, I looked first at the Hasbro execs, a few of whom were nodding in, if not agreement, consideration. I then turned to the players.

"Any comments on this?" I asked as I scanned the table.

I was greeted by blank faces and total silence. In retrospect, it reminds me of the vaudeville comedian peering out at a mute, unresponsive crowd and asking, "Is this an audience or an oil painting?"

A few more seconds passed. Then we moved on. To me, it had just been completely confirmed by the players that they wanted to do it on their own. Even now, five years later, I'm sure my motivation was mixed at best. Undoubtedly, part of me was making a last-minute attempt to keep my organization intact after more than twenty-five years. Hey, I'm only human. Another part of me sincerely felt an interim step would be good for all involved. Having been the person squarely in the middle between Hasbro and the players for so long, I knew there was going to be a lot of nuance, unanswered questions, unexplored mutual territory, and financial considerations. Some navigational experience could help. But it was not meant to be.

The rest of the meeting was a blend of questions and observations, both the theoretical and the practical. It was agreed that the players would take over all aspects of SCRABBLE clubs and tournaments. This would be itemized and signed off on in the coming months. The NSA would devote itself to getting as many new people playing as much SCRABBLE as often as possible. Oh yeah—and buying more games. Ultimately, it was agreed that the new players' organization—soon officially named the North American SCRABBLE Players Association—would take over all club and tournament activities on July 1, 2009.

As early as that evening, I'd processed and accepted the new structure. I had to admit that there were plenty of upsides to the change as well. For one thing, I'd no longer have to deal with some of the peskier, tedious, and unsettling aspects of the job.

The complaints from NSA members were at the top of the list. Believe me, I understood where they came from: a passion for the game and a naïveté about the business end of the NSA—not the least of which were legal, practical, and financial constraints under which we operated. The NSA also received thousands of letters, e-mails, and phone calls over the years, which would soon no longer be our responsibility. Perennial favorites included lost game pieces, new ideas for improving SCRABBLE, looking to license the SCRABBLE name, complaints about words, complaints about rude behavior on illegal Internet SCRABBLE sites, looking for donations, looking for NSA endorsements, needing information and/or permission to publish a SCRABBLE book, incarcerated people wanting to connect, foreign SCRABBLE associations seeking materials . . . the list goes on.

I cannot let this topic pass without sharing a bit about the number of people in prisons who passionately play SCRABBLE. For years, not a week passed when the NSA did not receive letters from the incarcerated asking for merchandise, rulings on a play or word, or the feasibility of starting a SCRABBLE club at the writer's penal institution.

I had, in fact, once been challenged to visit a prison to play its champion in a match. I thought it would be a cool experience, but

Hasbro felt otherwise. They must have felt that in its own way, it would have been as least as dangerous for me as appearing on *The Daily Show with Jon Stewart*.

The NSA once received a remarkable letter from an inmate recounting a fierce SCRABBLE game against another inmate. It detailed an argument that had ensued over the admissibility of a certain word in SCRABBLE. Things became so heated that the sender of the letter ended up stabbing his opponent in the eye with the pencil they'd been using to keep score.

The inmate even included a photocopy of the warden's official report for proof, which also revealed the prisoner had spent fifteen days in solitary confinement for the attack. The prisoner concluded the letter to us by insisting that if he'd had an *Official SCRABBLE Players Dictionary* none of this would have happened. Everybody's a victim, right? If we'd send him one, he said, this type of violence would be eliminated. But these guys got off easy. In 1983, according to the *Houston Chronicle*, thirty-one-year-old Anthony Dutton was stabbed to death by a fellow inmate at the El Paso county jail during an argument over SCRABBLE rules.

This kind of stuff would ultimately be the province of the North American SCRABBLE Players Association and Hasbro personnel. The NSA would now devote itself exclusively to outreach for the National School SCRABBLE Program, to initiatives with libraries, literacy groups, Scouts, parks and recreations departments, and the like, and to public relations and media.

We performed those duties from July 2009 until July 1, 2013. But while our change was happening, so were several things at Hasbro. Chief among these, as reported in various newspapers, was Hasbro's decision to consolidate most of its U.S. executives in one location: Rhode Island. So while the East Longmeadow, Massachusetts, Games Group would still manufacture the game, everything would be run out of Rhode Island. As these things often go in corporate America, this resulted in many resignations, firings, and transfers. Before long hardly anyone from the team of executives we'd been working with for twenty years at Hasbro Games was left at the company.

Going forward, the NSA and I would now be working with an entirely new group of corporate executives from Rhode Island. Early on, a few team members assigned to SCRABBLE left or were reassigned before we even met them or could get any traction. When we finally settled into our new team, there was one glaring thing that struck me: titles.

For most of my SCRABBLE career with Hasbro, our regular marketing meetings included Hasbro Games directors, vice presidents, senior vice presidents, and, often, the president of Hasbro Games. At our new meetings in Rhode Island, Hasbro was represented by a senior product manager, a director, and an assistant manager. In military terms, I'd gone from working with the generals and colonels to the lieutenants and captains. Don't get me wrong: they were smart and eager, and I liked them personally, but I'd gone from working closely with the power base and decision makers to, in many cases, never even meeting them. Instinct and experience told me that this did not bode well for the NSA, SCRABBLE, or me.

In the fall of 2012 the NSA staff and I did the dance with the new Hasbro regime. We mutually agreed that the National School SCRABBLE Program and attendant outreach would continue to be our focus, as the future of the game heavily relied on its success. As I'd done about every six months for the previous decade, I also urged Hasbro to ratchet up its SCRABBLE Internet presence and commitment in the following ways: create a safe School SCRABBLE site where kids could play as both individuals and as part of a school team. Consider online tournaments for both adults and kids. And, dammit, please fix the only official existing SCRABBLE app on Facebook.

That particular flaw had been bothering me since the day it was introduced. The flaw? You can play a fake word on the official Facebook SCRABBLE app and *not be penalized!* The phony word simply comes off the board, and you can keep trying until a word is good. This bugged me and other players for a number of reasons. First, it violates the most fundamental rule in SCRABBLE: a word has to be in the dictionary to be good in the game. Otherwise, it comes off the board and the player is penalized by missing a turn. This flaw also favors the weaker player. Think about it. People spend years improving their SCRABBLE arsenal of words, yet some newbie can walk in off the digital street and keep throwing letters out there until he or she gets a bingo. (I went to the SCRABBLE Facebook site the day I wrote this in 2014. Over decade later, this has not been corrected.)

But I really should not have been surprised. I remember going to Electronic Arts in Northern California a decade earlier to see the SCRABBLE Facebook app in its final stage of development before launch. Hasbro had granted EA the SCRABBLE license earlier, and everyone was under pressure to make the deadline.

After a demonstration from an enthusiastic team of young electronic gamers, I saw this and other aspects that seriously needed to be addressed. No one argued with my points; they were too obvious and valid. In frustration, I asked the team what

SCRABBLE experts had been involved in the research, design, and development of this new version. Everyone was quiet for a second; then someone muttered something along the lines of "One of our designers, Jeff, and his girlfriend are SCRABBLE *fanatics.* They play, like, almost every night."

I said nothing. I'd seen this movie before in my business experience. It's about, at the end of it all, the deal being more important than the execution. It often seemed more important to meet the contractual deadline—show me the money—than doing it right. God forbid you get the product the best it can be, then you launch it.

It was this kind of episode that made me incrementally realize I'd become a dinosaur in a game business and game world that was changing. I got the distinct impression that the new regime of Hasbro executives saw me as a pesky hybrid: SCRABBLE purist and, quite possibly, obstructionist. And I understood that. I'd once been an impatient young executive before my SCRABBLE career, fidgeting during meetings while some sixty-year-old fossil explained, "This is the way we've always done things."

In January of 2013, I knew it was time to go. We all did. After weeks of discussions, it became clear that my vision for the game's future and that of Hasbro were no longer the same. If I had any doubts, the reality of Hasbro's new vision was made clear in a conversation with a former digital games colleague who shared some interesting information.

We were talking about word games, and I was informed that Hasbro had bought the rights to make a Words with Friends board game based on the Internet sensation that many have written was actually ripped off from Hasbro's SCRABBLE itself.

My first thought was ego-driven. Geez, I used to be the first guy you called when the company was even considering anything about word games. Now I'm hearing about it as a fait accompli. Finally, I asked what was the thinking behind this move.

"Well," he told me, "we really wanted a SCRABBLE-type board game for the future, the next generation."

I remember thinking: You already have one, man. You already have one.

17

AFTER WORDS: AFTERWARDS

ULTIMATELY WE AGREED THAT THE National SCRABBLE Association after twenty-five years would be dissolved and we would turn our remaining activities over to NASPA and Hasbro marketing executives. July 1, 2013, would be our final day.

From the players' point of view, things were in good hands. Based in Dallas, NASPA is run by copresidents Christopher Cree and John Chew. This is an exceptional pair of individuals, whose personalities, skills, and experience are both impressive and complimentary.

Chris is a Texan, first and foremost. He's got a big personality, a small fortune, and a boundless heart. He's one of the most evolved men I know. Chris has been an extremely successful businessman in several areas and is widely respected both as a top player and as a person.

Years earlier, I'd named Chris as the NSA's first ombudsman, or player representative, at a time when many members were still dissatisfied with the communication between them and the NSA. It was a successful move on all sides, and Chris's contribution to the NSA and the game at large is inestimable. He's also served as an NSA Advisory Board member and was an NSA Person of the Year, a SCRABBLE All*Star, and a tireless organizer.

John Chew is an academic, with specialties in mathematics and computer programming. John is as self-effacing as Chris Cree is gregarious. He has pretty much overseen all official SCRABBLE activities in Canada for the past fifteen or more years, including running North America's oldest official SCRABBLE club and the Canadian National Championship, among other things. Like Chris, John is a top player who has played in the World SCRABBLE Championship, served on the NSA Advisory Board, and been an NSA Person of the Year. John also travels all over the world as a tournament consultant for other countries.

Together, these guys along with key volunteer staffers have done an amazing job carrying on many of the former NSA activities—especially considering we had substantial corporate funding and a paid staff. They've already proven that with successful and well-attended National SCRABBLE Championships and other initiatives.

As for the Hasbro side of things, it's hard for me to say. Figuratively, it's hard to say because I haven't spoken to a Hasbro person since late June 2013, and I don't really know the company's current and future plans for the game.

Fortunately—yet again—we have Stefan Fatsis. As he's done so often and so masterfully, Stefan has addressed this chapter in SCRABBLE history with both passion and perspective. Here, for the final word, is his article from the July 14, 2013, edition of the *New York Times*.

SCRABBLING OVER SCRABBLE

By Stefan Fatsis

After more than 25 years managing, marketing and refereeing the competitive side of America's most venerated word game, the National Scrabble Association has packed up its tiles and gone out of business.

Its demise doesn't reflect a lack of interest in Scrabble, which turns 65 this year. The game has never been more popular. More than a million people, from kids to hipsters to nonagenarians, play daily on Facebook. In May, nearly 200 students in fourth through eighth grades competed in the National School Scrabble Championship. On Saturday, more than 500 die-hards, myself included, will gather in Las Vegas for the National Scrabble Championship, a five-day, 31-game anagrammatic marathon.

Instead, the death of Scrabble's organizing body—which closed on July 1 following years of declining financial support from Hasbro, the game's owner—reflects a broader conflict between corporate and intellectual forces in American cultural life.

Guess which one is winning. Played at its highest level, Scrabble is a strategic sibling of chess, backgammon and the Chinese game go. Top tournament players must master as many of the 178,000 acceptable 2- through 15-letter words as possible, "see" them among a jumble of letters, determine which maximize the chances of winning and consider an opponent's possible countermoves, all while a timer ticks from 25 minutes to zero for each player to make all plays.

Like those old games, competitive Scrabble is a math-brain exercise, one combining spatial relations, board geometry and language maximization. Unlike them, it is owned by a company, whose goal is to generate revenue through the sale of sets and spinoffs and downloads.

"You have to understand that we are in the games-making business. We are not in the altruism business," a marketing executive for Selchow & Righter, Scrabble's first corporate parent, said during a meeting with tournament players lobbying for support in 1985. But those words could just as easily have been spoken last week by an executive of Hasbro, which has owned the rights to Scrabble in the United States and Canada since 1989.

During the past quarter-century, Hasbro has spent millions of dollars financing the independent National Scrabble Association. The association organized national, world and school championships; booked the winners on the "Today" show and "Jimmy Kimmel Live"; sanctioned more than 200 local tournaments a year; maintained a database of several thousand dues-paying players and calculated their tournament ratings; placed the game on ESPN for six straight years; published a newsletter; worked with Merriam-Webster on the official Scrabble dictionary (a fifth edition is in the works; get ready for "gi," "cuz," "ixnay" and more); and fielded inquiries ranging from disputatious living-room players seeking rules adjudications to a 1990s media blowup over the inclusion of the word "jew" in the lexicon.

Was that corporate money well spent? The publicity that the Scrabble association helped generate no doubt sold more than a few boards. But the group's performance could not and should not have been measured in such a reductive way.

Scrabble isn't a marketing or earnings-report star. It can't be hyped with an online vote resulting in a cat's replacing an iron, which Hasbro employed to juice sales of Monopoly. It doesn't rely on new cards that players need to buy to keep playing, like the Hasbro game Magic: The Gathering.

But as a game, Scrabble is remarkable. It carefully balances skill and luck and risk and reward. It exploits the breadth and beauty of the English language. It fosters mind-blowing creativity, heart-stopping tension and computer-stretching quantitative analysis.

Most people playing online or at the kitchen table aren't aware of Scrabble's complexity, let alone its tournament culture. Hasbro, obviously, is. The corporate question is whether it has a responsibility to both worlds, casual and competitive—and whether that responsibility extends to times like these, when Hasbro has been laying off workers and focusing on top-selling products.

Corporations from Coca-Cola to the N.F.L. are caretakers of some slice of history. Usually that history is central to the business. To Hasbro, Scrabble isn't. But it is an enduring piece of Americana, developed in a garden apartment in Jackson Heights, Queens, by an unemployed architect named Alfred Butts who spent years perfecting his game before it swept the country in the 1950s. I have yet to find a parallel for it—that is, a proprietary game with a subculture whose passion and sophistication transcend its ownership.

What's the value of that to a $4 billion corporation? Is it more or less than the $700,000 or $800,000 a year Hasbro spent on the National Scrabble Association at its peak—before it stopped paying for club and tournament Scrabble in

2008 and slashed the budget for school and casual Scrabble to the point that the association decided to cease operations.

But forget about money. What's the value of something like Scrabble to the culture at large? Does its owner have an obligation to nurture each side of the game, whether or not it jibes with the prosaic nature of the toy industry or boosts profits? Do history and intellect matter?

I spoke recently with Hasbro's chief marketing officer, John Frascotti. He said the right things about Scrabble's past and its competitive side. Hasbro is "committed to spending marketing dollars to promote the Scrabble brand and to promote Scrabble play," Mr. Frascotti said. He told me he believed the company could do what the Scrabble association did, at least for schools and casual players. "Judge us as we act, not as we say," he said.

I promised to keep an open mind. But since I started playing competitively and reporting on Scrabble 15 years ago, I've shaken hands with a moving walkway of Hasbro executives, all of whom have pledged love for and commitment to the game. And then the cuts came. Hasbro recently withdrew its last, token contribution to the national championship: $15,000 in prize money.

The winner of the tournament in Las Vegas will still be paid $10,000. After the company pulled the plug on them in 2008, competitive players formed their own governing body, the North American Scrabble Players Association, and, thanks to higher dues and participation fees, the tournament circuit has kept humming. If Hasbro does the same with School Scrabble—Mr. Frascotti said it wouldn't—I'll help find a way for my 11-year-old daughter and other young devotees to compete for a title in an educational game that they adore.

Hasbro knows that we players will volunteer to do what it had paid others to do for it: support a culture that doesn't necessarily fit in an earnings-driven world of fad toys and movie tie-ins. Maybe that's smart business. But with ownership comes responsibility, and sometimes even a little altruism.

Well said, Stefan.

It is now August 1, 2014. I recognize, accept, and occasionally savor my ongoing irrelevance in the world of SCRABBLE. I still play every day online against a dozen or so opponents. They range from some of the top players to casual players I've encountered along the way. The former NSA headquarters—an old sea captain's house in historic Greenport, New York—has had the sign removed and its files emptied. I still hear about the club and tournament scene, only now it's second- or thirdhand and often weeks later.

Remnants remain. This winter I started a wood-stove fire using a handful of old wooden racks as kindling. Mostly, though, it's tiles. For years, random letters have turned up everywhere— in pockets, in drawers, under furniture, on the floor of my car, in the yard. One day shortly after I resigned, I found two tiles in a corner in my attic. They were a z and an E. I knelt down and switched around them on the floor. E z. Yeah, I thought. E z. Yeah, EASY!

I knew everything was going to be okay.

APPENDIX

TOP TEN PLAYERS IN NORTH AMERICA AS OF JANUARY 1, 2015

Please see www.cross-tables.com for most current stats

1.	Nigel Richards	2141
2.	Adam Logan	2097
3.	David Gibson	2090
4.	Will Anderson	2061
5.	Mack Meller	2039
5.	Jesse Day	2039
7.	Ian Weinstein	2024
8.	Conrad Bassett-Bouchard	2023
9.	David Wiegand	2022
10.	Joel Sherman	2010

ANSWERS TO NSSC CONTEST ON PAGE 112

CERULEAN, SCHMOOZE, QWERTY, QUIXOTIC, HIJACK, ZYGOTE, SHEL-LAC, ZOOLOGY, INQUIRY, BAZAAR

ANSWERS TO ANAGRAMS ON PAGE 162

1. PYRIC = PRICY
2. CHURL = LURCH
3. TRADED = DARTED
4. SADDLE = ADDLES
5. RACOON = CORONA
6. NASTILY = SAINTLY
7. PAYOUTS = AUTOPSY
8. BEEFIER = FREEBIE
9. DROOLED = DOODLER
10. EXCLAIMS = CLIMAXES
11. SPAWNING = WINGSPAN
12. INDULGED = DELUDING

"OFFENSIVE" WORD LIST
REFERRED TO IN CHAPTER 4

Words removed from the *Official SCRABBLE Players Dictionary* in the mid-1990s because they were deemed offensive:

ABO	BADASS	BALLSY
ABOS	BADASSED	BAZOOMS
ARSE	BADASSES	BLOWJOB
ASSHOLE	BALLSIER	BLOWJOBS
ASSHOLES	BALLSIEST	BOCHE

BOCHES	CUNTS	FEMINAZIS
BOFFED	DAGO	FRIG
BOFFING	DAGOES	FRIGGED
BOINK	DAGOS	FRIGGING
BOINKED	DARKEY	FRIGS
BOINKING	DARKEYS	FUBAR
BOINKS	DARKIE	FUCK
BOLLOCKS	DARKIES	FUCKED
BOOBIE	DARKY	FUCKER
BOODIES	DICKED	FUCKERS
BOODY	DICKHEAD	FUCKING
BUBBA	DICKHEADS	FUCKOFF
BUBBAS	DICKING	FUCKOFFS
BUBBIES	DIKEY	FUCKS
BUBBY	DIPSHIT	FUCKUP
BUCKRA	DIPSHITS	FUCKUPS
BUCKRAS	DYKEY	GADJE
BULLDYKE	FAGGIER	GADJO
BULLDYKES	FAGGIEST	GANGBANG
BULLSHAT	FAGGOTRIES	GANGBANGS
BULLSHIT	FAGGOTRY	GAZOO
BULLSHITS	FAGGOTY	GAZOOS
BULLSHITTED	FAGGY	GINZO
BULLSHITTING	FART	GINZOES
COJONES	FARTED	GIRLIES
COLOREDS	FARTING	GOY
COMSYMP	FARTS	GOYIM
COMSYMPS	FATSO	GOYISH
CRAPPER	FATSOES	GOYS
CRAPPERS	FATSOS	GRINGA
CUNT	FEMINAZI	GRINGAS

GRINGO	JOHNSON	NOOKY
GRINGOS	JOHNSONS	OFAY
HAOLE	KANAKA	OFAYS
HAOLES	KANAKAS	PAPISM
HARDASS	KIKE	PAPISMS
HARDASSES	KIKES	PAPIST
HEBE	LES	PAPISTIC
HEBES	LESBO	PAPISTRIES
HONKEY	LESBOS	PAPISTRY
HONKEYS	LESES	PAPISTS
HONKIE	LEZ	PEED
HONKIES	LEZZES	PEEING
HONKY	LEZZIE	PISS
HOS	LEZZIES	PISSANT
HUNKEY	LEZZY	PISSANTS
HUNKEYS	LIBBER	PISSED
HUNKIE	LIBBERS	PISSER
HUNKIES	MERDE	PISSERS
JESUIT	MERDES	PISSES
JESUITIC	MICK	PISSING
JESUITRIES	MICKS	POM
JESUITRY	NANCE	POMMIE
JESUITS	NANCES	POMMIES
JEW	NANCIES	POMMY
JEWED	NANCY	POMS
JEWING	NIGGER	POO
JEWS	NIGGERS	POOED
JIGABOO	NITCHIE	POOFS
JIGABOOS	NITCHIES	POOFTAH
JISM	NOOKIE	POOFTAHS
JISMS	NOOKIES	POOFTER

POOFTERS	SHITHEAD	TOMMED
POOFY	SHITHEADS	TOMMING
POOING	SHITLESS	TURD
POONTANG	SHITLIST	TURDS
POONTANGS	SHITLISTS	TWAT
POOS	SHITLOAD	TWATS
POOVE	SHITLOADS	WANK
POOVES	SHITS	WANKED
POPERIES	SHITTED	WANKER
POPERY	SHITTIER	WANKERS
POPISH	SHITTIEST	WANKING
POPISHLY	SHITTING	WANKS
REDNECK	SHITTY	WAZOO
REDNECKS	SHKOTZIM	WAZOOS
REDSKIN	SHVARTZE	WETBACK
REDSKINS	SHVARTZES	WETBACKS
SHAT	SKIMO	WHITEYS
SHEENEY	SKIMOS	WHITIES
SHEENEYS	SPAZ	WILLIE
SHEENIE	SPAZZ	WOG
SHEENIES	SPAZZES	WOGGISH
SHEGETZ	SPIC	WOGS
SHICKSA	SPICK	WOP
SHICKSAS	SPICKS	WOPS
SHIKSA	SPICS	YID
SHIKSAS	SPIK	YIDS
SHIKSE	SPIKS	
SHIKSEH	SQUAW	
SHIKSEHS	SQUAWS	
SHIKSES	STIFFIE	
SHIT	STIFFIES	

IMPORTANT SHORT Q WORDS

QI	SUQ	QATS	QUAI	QUIN	QUOD
QAT	AQUA	QOPH	QUAY	QUIP	SUQS
QIS	QADI	QUAD	QUEY	QUIT	
QUA	QAID	QUAG	QUID	QUIZ	

2-LETTER WORDS FROM *OSPD5*

AA	AT	ED	GI	JO	MY	OP	SH	UT
AB	AW	EF	GO	KA	NA	OR	SI	WE
AD	AX	EH	HA	KI	NE	OS	SO	WO
AE	AY	EL	HE	LA	NO	OW	TA	XI
AG	BA	EM	HI	LI	NU	OX	TE	XU
AH	BE	EN	HM	LO	OD	OY	TI	YA
AI	BI	ER	HO	MA	OE	PA	TO	YE
AL	BO	ES	ID	ME	OF	PE	UH	YO
AM	BY	ET	IF	MI	OH	PI	UM	ZA
AN	DA	EX	IN	MM	OI	PO	UN	
AR	DE	FA	IS	MO	OM	QI	UP	
AS	DO	FE	IT	MU	ON	RE	US	

SHORT J WORDS FROM *OSPD5*

JO	JAR	JIB	JOT	JUT	DJIN
AJI	JAW	JIG	JOW	RAJ	DOJO
HAJ	JAY	JIN	JOY	TAJ	FUJI
JAB	JEE	JOB	JUG	AJAR	GOJI
JAG	JET	JOE	JUN	AJEE	HADJ
JAM	JEU	JOG	JUS	AJIS	HAJI

HAJJ	JAVA	JETE	JIVE	JOTS	JUPE
JABS	JAWS	JETS	JIVY	JOUK	JURA
JACK	JAYS	JEUX	JOBS	JOWL	JURY
JADE	JAZZ	JIAO	JOCK	JOWS	JUST
JAGG	JEAN	JIBB	JOES	JOYS	JUTE
JAGS	JEED	JIBE	JOEY	JUBA	JUTS
JAIL	JEEP	JIBS	JOGS	JUBE	KOJI
JAKE	JEER	JIFF	JOHN	JUCO	MOJO
JAMB	JEES	JIGS	JOIN	JUDO	PUJA
JAMS	JEEZ	JILL	JOKE	JUDY	RAJA
JANE	JEFE	JILT	JOKY	JUGA	SOJA
JAPE	JEHU	JIMP	JOLE	JUGS	SOJU
JARL	JELL	JINK	JOLT	JUJU	
JARS	JEON	JINN	JOOK	JUKE	
JATO	JERK	JINS	JOSH	JUKU	
JAUK	JESS	JINX	JOSS	JUMP	
JAUP	JEST	JIRD	JOTA	JUNK	

SHORT X WORDS FROM *OSPD5*

AX	FIX	MIX	REX	WAX	AXLE
EX	FOX	MUX	SAX	XIS	AXON
OX	GOX	NIX	SEX	ZAX	BOXY
XI	HEX	OXO	SIX	APEX	BRUX
XU	KEX	OXY	SOX	AXAL	CALX
AXE	LAX	PAX	TAX	AXED	COAX
BOX	LEX	PIX	TIX	AXEL	COXA
COX	LOX	POX	TUX	AXES	CRUX
DEX	LUX	PYX	VEX	AXIL	DEXY
FAX	MAX	RAX	VOX	AXIS	DOUX

DOXY	FALX	ILEX	MOXA	OXIC	SEXY
EAUX	FAUX	IXIA	NEXT	OXID	TAXA
EXAM	FIXT	JEUX	NIXE	OXIM	TAXI
EXEC	FLAX	JINX	NIXY	PIXY	TEXT
EXED	FLEX	LUXE	ONYX	PLEX	VEXT
EXES	FLUX	LYNX	ORYX	POXY	WAXY
EXIT	FOXY	MAXI	OXEN	PREX	XYST
EXON	HOAX	MINX	OXER	ROUX	
EXPO	IBEX	MIXT	OXES	SEXT	

SHORT Z WORDS FROM *OSPD5*

ADZ	ZIG	CZAR	JAZZ	QUIZ	ZEDS
AZO	ZIN	DAZE	JEEZ	RAZE	ZEES
BIZ	ZIP	DITZ	LAZE	RAZZ	ZEIN
COZ	ZIT	DOZE	LAZY	RITZ	ZEKS
CUZ	ZOA	DOZY	LUTZ	SIZE	ZEPS
FEZ	ZOO	FAZE	MAZE	SIZY	ZERK
FIZ	ZUZ	FIZZ	MAZY	TIZZ	ZERO
TIZ	ZZZ	FOZY	MEZE	TZAR	ZEST
WIZ	ADZE	FRIZ	MOZO	WHIZ	ZETA
ZA	AZAN	FUTZ	NAZI	YUTZ	ZIGS
ZAG	AZON	FUZE	OOZE	YUZU	ZILL
ZAP	BAZX	FUZZ	OOZY	ZAGS	ZINC
ZAS	BIZE	GAZE	ORZO	ZANY	ZINE
ZAX	BOZO	GEEZ	OUZO	ZAPS	ZING
ZED	BUZZ	GRIZ	OYEZ	ZARF	ZINS
ZEE	CAZH	HAZE	PHIZ	ZEAL	ZIPS
ZEK	CHEZ	HAZY	PREZ	ZEBU	ZITI
ZEP	COZY	IZAR	PUTZ	ZEDA	ZIZZ

ZITS	ZOIC	ZONE	ZOOM	ZOOS	ZOUK
ZOEA	ZONA	ZONK	ZOON	ZORI	ZYME

IMPORTANT VOWEL DUMPS

AA	ALEE	EAUX	LUAU	RAIA	AUDIO
AE	ALOE	EAVE	MEOU	ROUE	AURAE
AI	AMIA	EIDE	MOUE	TOEA	AUREI
OE	AMIE	EMEU	NAOI	UNAI	COOEE
OI	ANOA	EPEE	OBIA	UNAU	EERIE
EAU	AQUA	ETUI	OBOE	UREA	LOOIE
AEON	AREA	EURO	ODEA	UVEA	LOUIE
AERO	ARIA	IDEA	OGEE	ZOEA	MIAOU
AGEE	ASEA	ILEA	OHIA	AALII	OIDIA
AGIO	AURA	ILIA	OLEA	ADIEU	OORIE
AGUE	AUTO	INIA	OLEO	AECIA	OURIE
AIDE	AWEE	IOTA	OLIO	AERIE	QUEUE
AJEE	BEAU	IXIA	OOZE	AIOLI	URAEI
AKEE	CIAO	JIAO	OUZO	AQUAE	ZOEAE
ALAE	EASE	LIEU	QUAI	AREAE	

Q WITHOUT U WORDS FROM *OSPD5*

QI	QOPH	QANAT
QAT	CINQS	QIBLA
QIS	FAQIR	QOPHS
CINQ	NIQAB	TRANQ
QADI	QADIS	FAQIRS
QAID	QAIDS	NIQAAB
QATS	QAJAQ	NIQABS

QABALA	TRANQS	QWERTYS
QAJAQS	KAMOTIQ	SHEQELS
QANATS	NIQAABS	KAMOTIQS
QIBLAS	QABALAH	MBAQANGA
QIGONG	QABALAS	QABALAHS
QINDAR	QWWALI	QAWWALIS
QINTAR	QIGONGS	QINDARKA
QWERTY	QINDARS	SHEQALIM
SHEQEL	QINTARS	MBAQANGAS

IMPORTANT I DUMPS

BIDI	IMPI	IWIS	MINI	PILI
HILI	INIA	IXIA	MIRI	TIKI
IBIS	INTI	KIWI	NIDI	TIPI
ILIA	IRID	LIRI	NISI	TITI
IMID	IRIS	MIDI	PIKI	ZITI

USE THOSE U'S FROM *OSPD5*

ULU	GURU	KUDU	LULU	SULU	ULUS
BUBU	JUJU	KURU	MUMU	TUTU	UNAU
FUGU	JUKU	LUAU	PUPU	YUZU	URUS

TEN TIPS TO INSTANTLY
GET BETTER AT SCRABBLE

1. **Two- and Three-Letter Words.** Learn the 101 acceptable two- and three-letter words. They are the building blocks toward expert play and can boost your average score by as many as 50 points a game. They also create the opportunity for making multiple words on one move and finding additional places to play words by hooking onto or overlapping words already on the board.

2. **Secret of the s.** Use the s to pluralize an existing word to make two words at once. But use that s wisely. Don't use it on a move unless it gives you another 10-12 points. This doesn't apply if you have more than one s. Hint: should you have an extra s look for the suffixes NESS and LESS for a big-time play.

3. **Shuffle Tiles on Your Rack.** Shuffle the tiles on your rack frequently to find common letter combinations such as ING, ERS, PRE, RE, GHT, IES, EST, FUL, and more. As you do this, you'll be surprised how words will appear on your rack.

4. **Bonus Squares.** Always look for way to make plays using the bonus squares. Check especially for premium squares next to vowels.

5. **Consider Your Next Play.** A good SCRABBLE move is composed of what you put on the board to score and

what you leave yourself to work with on your rack. If you make a decent play for 28 points but leave a rack with VUUW, chances are your next several racks will be terrible. Go for a balance of vowels and consonants.

6. **"Bingos."** This is what tournament players call it when you use all seven tiles for a 50-point bonus. Again, look for common letter combinations. Over time, you should learn how to manipulate your rack to a bingo, especially if you have bingo-prone tiles such as the blank, S, E, R, A, T.

7. **q-without-u Words.** Words such as QI, QAT, QAID, and others are invaluable for both scoring and getting rid of the Q, as it's not a bingo-prone or particularly workable tile. A full list of these words is on pages 211–212.

8. **Look for Hooks.** "Hooks" are single letters that can be added to existing words to form other words. While the S is the most obvious, don't forget the Y, D, R, or E. Examples: HAND(Y), PLAN(E), CARVE(D), and MAKE(R).

9. **Choice of Plays.** Even if you have a great play, look for a better one. You'll be amazed at how often a second look around the board for options will yield an even better move than you'd planned. And, remember, the best SCRABBLE move is not always about the most points. You need to consider your "rack leave" as well as what opportunity your move might leave for your opponent.

10. **Attitude.** Remember that everyone draws bad tiles from time to time; it comes with the turf. Also remember that luck is a factor for both you and your opponent. SCRABBLE is supposed to be fun. Don't dwell on your mistakes.

CONTACT INFORMATION FOR NORTH AMERICAN SCRABBLE PLAYERS ASSOCIATION (NASPA)

For more information on tournaments and clubs, email NASPA —North American SCRABBLE Players Association—at info@ scrabbleplayers.org, visit www.scrabbleplayers.org, or mail PO Box 12115, Dallas, TX, 75225-0115.

CONTACT INFORMATION FOR SCRABBLE WORDBOOK OR AUTHOR MIKE BARON

Mike Baron, PO Box 2448, Corrales, NM 87048

ACKNOWLEDGMENTS

First and foremost, I'd like to thank all my colleagues and friends who worked over the years at and with the National SCRABBLE Association. It was always a team effort and could not have been accomplished without you. I'd especially like to thank the final team of Jane Ratsey Williams, Theresa Bubb, Katie Schulz Hukill, and Patty Hocker. Your energy and dedication to the game took us all over the world as one of the best NSA teams ever.

Many thanks to Will Menaker, my editor at Liveright/ W. W. Norton, for your insight, hard work, and patience in bringing *Word Nerd* to reality. And much gratitude to editor Bob Weill for his help and early appreciation of the project, as well as to copy editor India Cooper for making order out of chaos. Also much appreciation to Ken Weinrib and Neil Rosini for their legal expertise and guidance, as well as Norton counsel Laura Goldin. And so much appreciation to and admiration for my agent, Regula Noetzli, for her experience, vision, and energy over the years. *Word Nerd* could not have happened without you.

Special thanks to SCRABBLE players and friends Stefan Fatsis, Joe Edley, Mike Baron, and Robert Kahn for their suggestions and contributions to the manuscript. Special thanks also to Merriam-Webster's John Morse for his friendship, encouragement, and contributions. Much appreciation as well to my colleagues at Merriam-Webster—Peter Sokolowski, Meghan Lungi, Jim Lowe, and Jane Mairs.

Of course, this book—and more importantly my SCRABBLE experience—could not have happened without my many colleagues at the Hasbro Games division in East Longmeadow, Massachusetts. Your confidence in our work and willingness to try new ideas over the decades helped introduce millions of new players to the world's greatest game.

ABOUT THE AUTHOR

John D. Williams Jr. was the executive director of the National SCRABBLE Association (NSA) and national spokesperson for the game for twenty-five years. He has been a tournament SCRABBLE player and publisher of the *SCRABBLE News* and is coauthor of the game's best-selling strategy book *Everything SCRABBLE*®. Among other achievements, Williams was a cofounder of the World SCRABBLE Championship, an architect of the acclaimed National School SCRABBLE Program and School SCRABBLE Championship, and creator of the SCRABBLE All*Stars, the United States' first televised SCRABBLE match. Under his leadership, the NSA raised over a million dollars in prize money for competitors and grew the tournament scene to over two hundred official competitions annually.

Williams has also worked as a writer and producer for both television and film for Nickelodeon, CNN, ESPN, Paramount, TV Land, and MTV Networks, among others. He lives in Greenport, New York, with his wife and business partner, Jane Ratsey Williams.